The Man Who Saw *the* Sun

and Other Plays

The Man Who Saw *the* Sun

and Other Plays

Makarand Sathe

SPEAKING TIGER

SPEAKING TIGER PUBLISHING PVT. LTD
4381/4 Ansari Road, Daryaganj,
New Delhi–110002, India

Published as a paperback by Speaking Tiger 2018

ISBN: 978-93-87693-47-0
eISBN: 978-93-87693-48-7

10 9 8 7 6 5 4 3 2 1

Typeset in Garamond Premier Pro by SÜRYA, New Delhi

Printed at
Sarat Impressions Pvt. Ltd., Kolkata

To Gajanan Paranjape

Contents

Introduction

In the summer of 1973, a large bunch of theatre practitioners of all ages descended on Pune's Film Institute for a unique ten-day workshop of structured and unstructured exchange. During the day, a group of young playwrights—selected for the promise they had shown—read out their plays. Some of the plays were complete and some were works-in-progress. After the readings, critics and senior practitioners who were present by invitation, discussed them threadbare. The exercise was meant to help the young playwrights understand what had worked in their plays, what had not and why. After these constructive and largely helpful discussions, the participants spent the evenings watching films sourced from the National Archives next door. The late evenings, as behoves theatre gatherings, were devoted to quaffing spirits and having spirited conversations about the day's events. This historic workshop was organized by theatre director-actor-writer-translator Satyadev Dubey as part of his two-year Homi Bhabha Fellowship project.

Twelve years later, playwright-director-actor Satish Alekar, who had read one of his early plays at the workshop, persuaded the Ford Foundation to make a grant to Pune's

Theatre Academy of which he was a founding member, to support a playwriting workshop for the next generation of playwrights. This workshop was also held in Pune, but in three stages, spanning the years between 1985 and 1987. The Ford Foundation grant also supported the production of some of the plays. Makarand Sathe was one of twelve playwrights selected for this workshop. The play he read was later directed by Vijay Kenkre. In an interview with this writer (*Playwright at the Centre: Marathi Drama From 1843 to the Present*, Seagull Books, 2000), Sathe said his response to the general run of plays on the Marathi stage, whether commercial or experimental, had been lukewarm. Alekar's plays were the only ones to which he had responded. Then a festival of Ionesco's plays came to the city and he realized this was the theatre he felt closest to. The play that made him really sit up was the Marathi adaptation of *The Bald Prima Donna*. My guess is, this was *Takkal Padleli Sundari*, adapted and brilliantly directed by Meena Deshpande, daughter of veteran playwright-journalist P.K. Atre.

The affinity Sathe felt for absurd theatre is not to be taken as an endorsement of the absurdist label that was stuck to his work in the early years. The labelling was no more than a nervous reaction by critics who were not sure what to make of it. The label stood in place of real understanding. Needless to say, Sathe's plays were not absurdist by any stretch of imagination. They did not emerge from the political-intellectual history that underpinned absurdism in Europe. They were not about the meaninglessness of life, but rather about the meaning that could be derived from the diverse factors that impinged upon and affected life. While following this path of exploration, Sathe created forms of theatre in which the rules of everyday logic were often disregarded. This bore a distant relationship to the absurdist method. But whereas the characters in absurdist plays spoke in short spurts and comical non sequiturs with no desire to communicate, Sathe's characters were necessarily articulate because they were carriers of ideas. The ideas came from his wide reading of philosophy and political theory, his socio-political concerns, his sense of history and his speculations about issues like the psycho-sociological impact of modern technology on society.

The play he had read at the Theatre Academy workshop brought together some of these concerns. *Charshe Koti Visarbhole*, later translated by Jayant Deshpande as *Four Hundred Forgetfuls* (Seagull Books, 1998), was Sathe's first full-length play. It explored the notion of eternal time and how the immortality granted to some of our mythological characters could be seen in its context. How, for instance, would the modern notion 'time is money' play out against the background of eternal time and immortality? Who would then be the rich and who the poor? Such conundrums were far from the questions that generally drove his contemporaries' plays, and further still from the expectations that the Marathi audience brought to the theatre. Consequently, this play and its successors were deemed 'difficult'. Even directors did not appear to have fully grasped their import, mode or language. So, what was dense on the page remained dense on the stage. *Chowk* (*Crossroads*) was an exception to the bafflement that some of Sathe's plays had produced. To begin with, it was not speculative but based on observed reality. More importantly, the production, directed by Sathe himself in conjunction with his long-time associate Atul Pethe, carried the play's multiple arguments with an ease that came from understanding them and thereby making them immediately comprehensible to the audience. I had not realized how complex the interwoven narratives were and how long and convoluted the narrator's interventions, till I translated the play and asked Sathe if the stage version had been drastically edited. He told me it had not.

When the country made its leap into a liberalized economy in the early 1990s, it impacted the psychological constitution of the individual and society. Neither remained an internally consistent, singular, integrated entity. Individuals were now fragmented into multiple identities which were not necessarily in dialogue with each other or with the surrounding world. Sathe had theorized this idea first in an extended essay titled *Dwidha* ('Divided'), then fictionalized it in his novel, *Achyut Athavale Ani Athvan* (*The Man Who Tried to Remember*, tr. Shanta Gokhale, Penguin Books, 2012), and dramatized it in *Chowk*. These diverse forms had allowed Sathe to view the problem of identity from different angles. The essay presented an argument, the novel posed questions about the role of the intellectual in a fragmented society, and the play precipitated a conflict of identities brought about by a situation that had trapped them in a single place—a traffic jam. Achyut Athavale, the chief protagonist of Sathe's novel, is back in *Chowk*, caught in the dilemma of the liberal thinker who is expected to articulate a consistent position on socio-economic issues but is unable to do so because he, more than anybody else, sees the validity of several positions simultaneously. His companion on the bus in which he is travelling to deliver one of his talks is Pratap Chavan, who has lost his job and wants a simple answer to help him understand the crisis he faces. Who is his enemy? Whom can he blame for his predicament? Athavale can only offer him a set of diverse narratives, each with its own validity depending on which angle you use to view the situation.

The play is structured like the Maharashtrian sweet champakali, also made in Bengal as elo jhelo. It comprises strips of pastry stuck together at one end, which fan out and separate in the middle and come together again at the other end. Similarly, *Chowk* begins with two broad identities of people—the violent and the non-violent. The traffic jam in which they are caught reveals how these identities are subdivided into multiple others. When the situation escalates into physical conflict, the many come together as two again—the violent and the non-violent.

The earliest of the three plays in this collection, *Surya Pahilela Manus* (*The Man Who Saw the Sun*), is an inquiry into truth and justice. It upholds Socrates' philosophy in which these values are posited as a means to a better society and as an end in themselves. The stage here is a little less crowded than in *Chowk* but much more so than in *Te Pudhe Gele* (*They Went Ahead*) which has, effectively, only two characters. Sathe has often played around with time and space. In *The Man Who Saw the Sun*, both are fluid. Time moves seamlessly between the present and the fifth century BCE and the space is, at one moment an imaginary cave, and the next, an imagined Athens. The characters too inhabit two times. There is a group of nameless men who belong to a fictional present and there are Plato, Socrates, Krito, Alcibiades, Phaedo and Xanthippe who belong to the historical past. The sun of the title is symbolic of truth. People who dwell voluntarily in dark caves take the shadows they see there for truth. When they see the sun by accident or design, they are blinded by its brilliance. However, they soon get used to it. It is then that they must choose whether to remain in the uncompromisingly clear light of truth or return to the murky shadows of the cave. Few choose the first. Most prefer the comfort of the latter.

Socrates lived his life under the sun, on the streets and in the public squares of Athens. Here he engaged young students in his unique method of inquiry, elenchus, in which he broke down the problem at hand—whether truth, justice, good or evil—into a series of sharply focused questions that eventually led to the answer they were seeking. The Socrates we know is the figure created by Plato from facts injected with his own idealism. We know nothing of him at first hand because he wrote nothing. Sathe's chief source of narrative material is therefore Plato's *Dialogues*. In the production of the play directed by Atul

Pethe, Socrates' speech made before the Senate in self-defence became the majestic centrepiece. The brilliance of the argument which led his accusers into sticky corners was its first strength, but Dr Shreeram Lagoo's towering performance was the second. Inflecting his deep, resonant voice to express every nuance of each word, Lagoo brought to his performance something even more valuable—the personal conviction of a man who had spent a lifetime fighting for reason against cant.

The most recent play of the present trio, which together make up about a fourth of Sathe's total oeuvre (as far as theatre is concerned; he has till date written three novels, many articles and theatre history as well), presents the dilemma of the liberal intellectual standing on the brink of a critical decision. The space here is limbo-like and the situation a matter of either/or. Progress lies out of sight just round the corner. But it appears that in order to get there, the poor—represented by the farmer couple lying in the background—must be exploited. The metaphor for exploitation is rape. That is what a group of people who were there when the intellectual arrives have done in order to go ahead. If the unnamed intellectual's own moral and ideological qualms prevent him from doing the same, he will have to stay put. That would spell stagnation. Here we have a third avatar of Achyut Athavale from *The Man Who Tried to Remember* and *Crossroads*. Soon a simple man with no intellectual pretensions arrives and wants to know where he is and what happens next. In the process of discussing the pros and cons of alternatives available to them, the intellectual wriggles out of his own dilemma. The new arrival is like Pratap Chavan of *Chowk*, looking for simple answers. He listens in bemusement to the convoluted mental gymnastics the intellectual performs, using history, politics and sociology to bolster his arguments. The new arrival asks, 'Isn't there an easy way out of all this?' The implied answer is no, not if you want to fool yourself into believing you have no option but to join the crowd. And so the intellectual rapes the farmer's wife and goes ahead. It is a shocking end. I remember asking Sathe after the show why he had found it necessary to spell out the act in all its brutality. He said something to the effect that, whereas in Tendulkar's time a knock was enough to shake the audience out of its complacency, today the impact of a truck was required to achieve the same effect.

In its central preoccupation, *Te Pudhe Gele* echoes Sartre's *No Exit* and Beckett's *Waiting for Godot*. It creates a situation designed to test the readiness or ability of the protagonists to exercise choice. In *No Exit*, the three characters locked in a single chamber after death, get so hopelessly entangled with each other in a drama of lust and redemption, that they cannot escape even when the door swings open. In *Waiting for Godot*, Vladimir and Estragon have the freedom to walk out of the space where they are waiting for Godot. Indeed, Estragon does leave each night, but inevitably returns in the hope that Godot will show up. The tramps have a choice, but only in theory. In practice, hope robs them of it. Unlike these characters, the intellectual of *Te Pudhe Gele* does move, but the movement is into a no-exit situation, like the mouse that smells the cheese and walks into the trap from which there is no escape. The central question the play poses is, how much are we willing to stake to hold on to a real, rather than an illusory freedom of choice?

The theatre of ideas is almost by definition word-heavy as are Sathe's plays. Most contemporary actors are not accustomed to delivering long speeches with dictional clarity. It is a handicap that makes directors nervous, resulting in their allowing actors to scramble through lines. Gajanan Paranjpe, Sathe's regular actor, has the intellectual and histrionic ability to do full justice to his idiom, tackling Sathe's rather unusual syntax and humour with understanding. As a translator I remember failing to find the right register for one of Sathe's early plays which I had agreed to translate. It was one of the few translation projects that I had to give up before I even started. I was happy to make up for that lapse with *Chowk* and part of *Surya Pahilela Manus* which I have translated for this volume.

Makarand Sathe is a political playwright in a culture that has not produced too many of them. There was G.P. Deshpande before him and arguably B.V. (Mama) Warerkar before Deshpande. People harbour the mistaken notion that plays which show the venality of politicians are political. The Marathi audience enjoys that kind of theatre. It does not welcome the theatre of ideas, nor plays that are as uncompromisingly experimental in form and substance as Sathe's are. That is the chief reason why many of Sathe's plays, like G.P. Deshpande's before him, have not enjoyed popular acclaim. Sathe rues the fact that even the younger generation of playwrights do not write from deep political convictions or a sense of history. It was this concern that prompted him to embark on a research project that culminated in what might be considered his magnum opus—the three-volume *Marathi Rangbhumichya Tees Ratri: Ek Samajik Rajkiya Itihas*, translated into English as *A Socio-Political History of Marathi Theatre: Thirty Nights* (OUP 2015). The history is written as a series of conversations between a clown and a playwright conducted on top of a hill in Pune over thirty nights. The clown largely represents Sathe's viewpoint. His unnamed interlocutor represents the pre-millennial generation of Marathi playwrights. Sathe's argument, supported by voluminous evidence, is that Marathi theatre has had a history of socio-political theatre. Why then has it not continued into contemporary times? Perhaps the answer may be found in *Chowk*. Multiple identities are not conducive to consistent political positions from which one may look at the world.

Shanta Gokhale
19 February 2018

THEY WENT AHEAD

Translated from the original Marathi play *Te Pudhe Gele*
by Ajay Joshi and Makarand Sathe

[In his late forties, an urban, spectacled, middle-class man, A, is sitting in a semi-nude state. He gets up with a start, and puts on the clothes lying around. He walks about restlessly, and looks around time and again, as if waiting for someone. His face shows the somewhat arrogant realization that he is an intellectual. In the background, two unknown people, a man and a woman, are sleeping on the floor in the darkness. {It is not necessary for them to be physically present, but a mattress and blankets can be arranged to indicate they are asleep.} A turns and looks at them now and then, as if twitchy at their presence. Another man enters. This man, B, is a middle-class city dweller in his early forties, and looks somewhat hassled. A quickly steps forward and pulls him under the spotlight. The stage is partly lit. The entire play takes place in tight spots. Circles of extreme bright light follow the action. The surrounding areas are pitch dark.]

A: Come...come in. Come here please...[*In a tone that a shopkeeper in a small marketplace would call out to a buyer, beckoning him to his shop. A realizes this. As a result he is a bit awkward. Still, he persists in his efforts.*] You are an Indian, right? Marathi? [*B hesitates.*]... Yes, Marathi. I realized that as soon as I saw you. I was nearly convinced... and you were mumbling something to yourself. [*B looks down, abashed.*] No, no, don't worry. I like people who mutter to themselves. Even I talk to myself, na! Someone who talks to himself considers all aspects of an issue. [*Now B has completely stopped in his tracks.*] Come, please, come inside. Good, now sit... So you were mumbling something. I couldn't follow what it was. But the words were in Marathi...which is great! I wanted just that kind of a man. Perfect. [*Bewilderment and doubt on B's face.*] No... No, I mean I wanted somebody like you...for communication... brotherhood...otherwise just about anyone could have come here, isn't it? You're aware that this place is like that. It feels good to have someone like yourself, like your kin. Sit, please sit... Oh, no, don't be scared. For one, I am not one of them. I mean one of those who you met on your way here. Now, what would you call them? Servants...or administrators or...well, it is difficult...huh...forget who they are...what is important is that I am not one of them. At least if you look at it from the point of view of our world...I mean the previous one... Even then, the two of us are like...what do they say? Birds of the same feather... [*B tries to say something. A stops him.*] No, no! There is no need to introduce yourself. It is quite clear that you are a Maharashtrian. Your clothes tell me you are middle class and urban. Your face says the same thing. The twist of your lips, the way in which surprise flits across your face...and you still haven't sat down. It means you are judging me, trying to decide whether to stay or leave. It means you think before you act...you don't make hasty decisions... Look at your hands, just look at them. [*Grasping his hand, A pulls him closer under the spotlight.*] Just like mine—delicate and soft. Your finger and toenails are neatly trimmed and moisturized. Your face looks polished...how suave you are! You're a good man...just like me. That's enough for us to come together... Oh! It's only me doing the talking. And I can see that you're annoyed... But this urge of mine to talk to you...this...your muttering to yourself...what else could it mean? We're birds of the same feather...[*B gets up to leave.*] Sir! Please...please do wait. Don't you think I look just like you...see, like this...? But I am talking again...I'm sorry...sit, please do sit. [*B sits down.*] Now speak.

[Pause]

A: Go on. Speak. How are you?

B: I'm fine.

[Pause. B looks beyond A's shoulders at the two sleeping figures. Realizing this, A promptly gets up and stands between B and the sleeping figures. A is a little frightened, his face both guilty and restless.]

A: No, don't worry about them...they won't do a thing. They're harmless, absolutely harmless. They too are Maharashtrians...but they're not like us. In fact they don't even talk, unless they are forced to. I've spent days with them. Believe me Sir, I defended them for so many days, just as if I was their lawyer.

B: You mean...you're a lawyer...

A:[*Smirking*] Yes, in a way... I am a lawyer by profession... but when I said I defended them...I meant their being here...in this place...

B: Here? You mean even here—

A: No, this is not a court. This is not a place that doles out justice...but it's close, very close. Still...you don't get 'justice' as you would think of it in the literal sense. This place is rather weird, the unexpected happens here... [*B gets up. A restrains him.*] Please don't leave. Wherever you go, the result will be the same. At least here you have the company of a like-minded person...quite similar...forget caste and religion...let all that be... I will talk of that later... The point is that I need you. You are useful to me. I know you are a good man, like most of us. You need proof? Let me explain... Take for example...during the tsunami you must have donated money to the relief fund. And very often you must have gone out of your way to help senior citizens and the blind to cross busy roads. You are a socially conscious person, just like me. You still want more proof? You must be philanthropic... I know. Yes, sir! People like us don't speak of such things openly... Finding time despite my hectic schedule, I defended poor clients and fought on behalf of NGOs for low fees...cases which were socially important... That apart, just look at you...it's so clear that whoever you may be... I mean whatever caste, religion, occupation...you have some intellectual social interest in this world... Do you watch a play or two? Read newspapers or Shekhar Gupta's editorials in the *Indian Express*... Magazines? Which ones? *India Today*? *Frontline*?

B: Not that. *India Today*, yes. That's better...

A: Look, didn't I tell you? You will definitely help me. In fact, we need each other. Now tell me. How are you?

B: Fine.

[B looks restless. He looks at the two at the back again. A is now very agitated.]

A: Sir! Don't look that way. Didn't I tell you they do nothing? You will see lakhs of people all over the place like these...even here, if you look carefully! It's we who are in the minority! That's why we must cling to each other... Just ignore them...as if they don't exist... Why is that so difficult? They are asleep. Let them sleep. They sleep a lot... And just in case they wake up, don't be terrified... If they wake up I will speak to you in English or then maybe in Hindi... They don't know a word of any language but Marathi... I'm telling you they're not like us... Bloody shit... This place is weird anyway, and on top of that if you keep looking there, it'll make things worse! Listen, I'm going to tell you about something that happened here...and you... [*B is restless.*] Sit, please sit.

[Pause]

A: Huh, See... Let me assure you of one thing. I wish you well. Look here, if I don't do this, you'll suffer the same fate as me. Then a terrible guilt will eat into you. Guilt makes life unbearable... We are suspended in limbo, you see...see, it's we who are affected... In this place it's we who brood and die...people like them will sleep like this...and the remaining bastards move ahead... It is sensitive people like us who get trapped. Are you a sensitive person? Huh? Are you?

B: Yes...I mean...I think I am. [*Again he aglances towards the back.*]

A: [*Yelling*] *Don't* look at them! [*Momentary pause. He controls himself with difficulty.*] See, I'll try and explain. But mind you...I'm in a hurry... I'm tired of these hardships... can't take it any more...I don't want to wait... Do you understand? I know you're sensitive, you can understand. I'll try to explain everything briefly and properly. But like a person completely shattered, suspended at the edge of an abyss, a person with self-contempt, helpless because of human limitations, my talk is bound to go a bit off track. [*Now he is very restless, nearly breaking down towards the end.*] Even after death, look what destiny has in store for us! For us middle-class simpletons! See, people like us must cling on to each other...don't you understand?

[B, though a little apprehensive, gets up, puts his hands on A's shoulders to comfort him. A grasps his hand firmly. B frees his hand from his clasp. Gently patting him, he goes back to his place. A is now composed.]

A: Thank you, I feel better now...sorry... How are you?

B: I'm fine.

A: Don't you feel restless?

B: I do...a bit.

A: Relax... Sit back. There's no hurry here.

[Pause]

B: What did you die of?

A: Accident.

[Pause]

A: You?

B: Heart attack.

[Pause]

B: [*Looking back*] And these two...

A: [*Again irritably*] Just leave them alone, will you? I will tell you about them. But only after a while. Have patience... OK? First tell me something. Did you fill up a form on your arrival...at that first place? That small place like a closet...with that person sitting at a table? And in front of his table, a smaller one, for us to sit on and complete the form?

B: Yes, I did fill up the form.

A: What did they ask? Name? Place?

B: No.

A: Occupation?

B: Nothing of that sort.

A: They only asked you to write twenty lines about yourself, didn't they?

B: Yes. And I wrote just that...name, occupation, address, children, likes and dislikes, what else could I write? So they—

A: Tore it to pieces? Correct. Then what did you write the second time?

B: Briefly from my childhood to...

A: History! They tore it too, your history was torn... Sir, they know all that... Then, after this happened a couple of times, you handed back a blank form. Correct?

B: I simply don't understand...what do they want from us?

A: Forget it. We don't have the time. I just want to know whether you have come here through specific channels. See, finally, will Man ever be able to unravel the secrets of the universe?

B: Right. And the irony is that even if people decipher it, it may become more difficult to live!

A: Why do you speak of facing life? Don't you realize that we are now dead, once and for all?

B: You're right. But it doesn't feel the same. This is an entirely different feeling—I mean from what we imagine what it would be like after dying.

A: So do you believe in it? What happens after death according to this religion or that...but first tell me...do you grieve when you remember your wife and kids?

B: Not at all! That's what I'm trying to tell you. I had a feeling it would happen this way, but...

A: That's because of the second chamber. Second place! Intense purple light, lit circles, thumping sounds...it felt like an MRI or a CT scan, right? You stand in that light, and some of our common feelings simply freeze. I mean they don't die, they just freeze—all those feelings about wives, children and parents left behind, or all those unfulfilled cravings... Correct?

B: Absolutely right! But why? If it was to be this way, then why keep those memories alive?

[Pause]

A: Since coming here I have thought about it a lot. You know what I think? I think they want to keep us as we were. The same as when we lived our earlier lives. But... but now, after we are dead, those memories elicit entirely different feelings... We no longer behave as we did when we were alive. We change...they may not want it to happen that way! Those bloody bastards... [*Pause*] But 'THEY' means who?... Shit! Whom do you trust?

B: Wasn't that precisely what they asked in the third chamber? Do you have faith? What kind of a fucking question. I told them I believed in—

A: Let that be, I got what I wanted. Now it is confirmed that we came here by the same route as the life we led. It's not like the earlier ones. Horrifying things happen here. Just thinking about it makes my hair stand on end. This place strips you of everything. Then decisions have to be taken. It makes you act. Waiting too long without action and submitting blank forms just doesn't help. You'll realize that now that you are so restless. How will you manage yourself here, huh?

[B gets up and struggles to get out of the confines of the lit area around him. A follows to catch hold of him. B leaps ahead. But he can't get out of the light, in spite of repeated attempts. A, who had tried to hold him back out of fear, now eases off.]

A: [*Fearfully*] Don't...don't go anywhere... Wherever you go...it's the same... Look! Look outside...believe me...at least here we have each other for company... [*B, realizing that he can't go outside, gives up. A relaxes.*] Huh...you can't go outside, can you? It's been more than ten minutes. You had ten minutes to make a choice. Now you're stuck here. Sit down.

[There is a pause after the struggle. B is still standing.]

A: Do one thing. Take a deep breath. And thank your luck that I'm around...this place is weird. Strange things happen here. But from what happens here, on those historic facts, our progress is decided...understood? I haven't a clue what lies ahead...because I don't believe in religion, God and such things. Chitragupta, Kayamat... Apocalypse and the rest...I don't think they exist. But here, I've realized we will get justice. See, I am a lawyer. I can recognize the tell-tale signs... But don't involve yourself in these matters. It's not easy to follow these structures...and I have my experiences, right? See, I'm a unique person. I have gone through what happened here once, and I am going through it again—how often does one get a chance to go through the present more than once? To amend history itself? And who gets a chance—[*B looks at the two at the back. A again gets irritated and nearly charges at him.*] Bastard! How often have I told you not to look at them? [*Pause. Deliberately steadies himself.*] OK! Yes, even they have been around here for some time. They too got the chance...to pass through the same situation again. And the fear is that they might behave differently this time. But... but I know it won't happen that way. To take advantage of such historic opportunities, you need privileged people like us...with our kind of background. [*Momentary pause.*

B faints. A holds him and gets him to sit down.] Sit, please sit. See, actually I am trying to help you. I too am a very, very sensitive man...just like you. Usually you have to wait here for a long time, a long, long time. But I am going to steer you through quickly. I have been through it once, you see! Let me tell you that history. Then we can learn from it. You will, won't you?

B: Yes! Otherwise history repeats itself. Those who don't learn from history make the same mistakes again.

A: [*Flaring up*] What do you mean, history repeats itself? Marx himself has already stated that. But that statement is of no use to us. Because now we have understood that it isn't that straightforward. [*Pause. Restless with memories, A yells.*] History doesn't teach us a thing! It only punishes us because we don't learn from it, that's all! Understood?

B: Why are you shouting? I'll do what you ask of me...

A: I don't want you to do it because I say so. Then it will lose its purpose. It doesn't happen that way here. I want you...to do what I ask you to do, ON YOUR OWN. And that is a difficult thing. [*Pause*] Anyway forget it, forget everything... Let's do it this way, let's first calm down. Now, pay attention to what I have to say. Take a deep breath... release. Good, how do you feel now?

B: Relaxed.

A: Don't be scared, tell the truth. I won't shout.

[Pause]

A: Come on, tell me...

B:It's like this, what will happen next... I mean that—I am waiting for something... I mean I feel that way... But I don't know why...because of which... I feel restless.

A: Correct. This is like the life we lived, keep that in mind. The same thing happened to us. It started the same way. [*Gets up, turns, and looks behind.*] When I came here, of these two, this gentleman was already present... Now I can't avoid talking about them. Let your curiosity be satisfied for once. This gentleman's name is Khanduji. Khanduji Kale. He—[*A stops mid-sentence, as if immersed in his thoughts, and comes forward and sits with his head down. Pause*]

B: Then?

A: Then what?

B: What of Khanduji Kale?

A: He died.

B: That's obvious. But of what?

A: He committed suicide.

B: Oh! I see. So that's what you meant when you said they were not like us. Why did they commit suicide? A jilted love affair?

A: No.

B: Less marks in higher secondary exams? Share market? I tell you it's stupid to commit suicide. Even I put in my stakes in the share market. But I always took precautions.

I played within my limits, you see... I mean one should always play within one's limits.

A; He didn't die because of the share market...he is a farmer.

B: Farmer...huh...then why did he... Oh! Oh!

A: Yes! He is a farmer. And he committed suicide. The rest we already know. Loans, cotton, daughter's wedding, moneylenders...

B: No...I mean, yes! Meaning actually I don't know the details. I...meaning I know that many farmers are committing suicide. But I don't know the intricacies involved. Anyway, so he is one of them, is he? I mean one of those farmer suicides we hear about all the time? In that case I want to see him. [*Gets up and heads towards the back. A grabs him and pulls him back.*]

A: Sit here, sit. I can understand your curiosity. But their waking up at this point will not be convenient for us... For once listen to what I have to say.

B: You tell me all about that, but...and you do appear to know about various things... I can imagine...a while ago you even had important information on Marx, and so I ask...can't we find a simple solution? I mean—

A: Don't you think it's too late now?

B: Yes, but isn't it alarming that so many people are committing suicide... I mean we can't do anything...but I ask just out of curiosity. I know a little...but I am always interested in knowing about things. A lot of social work is done in India now. The RSS activists even work among the Adivasis, that's what I read in *India Today*. Do you—

A: [*Annoyed*] Look here. I am not one of them. I believe in secularism. Whatever this Sangh activism did in Gujarat against the Muslims...

B: Exactly! I agree. Caste, creed is all humbug... The same for religion... One should have respect for all religions...I agree. But at least after death—

A: We are already dead... There is no time to discuss all this now. It's pointless. Listen to what happened next... So when I came here, I saw this Khanduji. I came to know him, and since I was well aware of the nitty-gritty of all these problems...you can imagine how sympathetic I felt. I was trying to make him speak...but it's difficult—he doesn't speak easily with people like us—

B: Why?

A: He feels...but leave that. What happened is more important. As I was trying to convey this to him, a group of eight to ten people barged in. All men from the same workplace...middle-level managers from the same company. Two were youngsters. The others were middle-aged and some could pass off as elderly. But what is more important is that all of them were mostly like us. Suddenly I felt relieved. I introduced Khanduji to them. All of them were sorry. Just like you. Now I won't get into details about all of them. Of the lot, two were believers. Another one was an economist, financial advisor...an atheist like me. It was he and I who gave the information to the others—about this farmer and his woes. [*While he presents the following theory, looking pleased with himself, his face assumes an expression of the moral high ground.*] We clearly presented both sides of the situation. I mean at one end: poverty, the condition of agricultural practices, exploitation, globalization, American subsidy...and at the other: the mad scamper of farmers to shift from traditional crops like jowar and bajra to cash crops like cotton, increasing their expectations, the global market, capitalism... And on the third front: new technologies—yes, and also about how the entire system is changing, how we are progressing on the social and economic fronts, how attitudes are changing as one moves from the agricultural system of production to industrialization and its compulsions. But in spite of all this, what was equally important was that people mustn't die. So why is there no alternative? You observe England from the middle of the eighteenth century to the Second World War. [*B is now listening, awestruck.*] Look at Europe, look at America. Consider Japan till the Second World War. It is a DARK period, a period of hardships for the poor. There is no way out. It happened to them earlier, and now it is happening with us. It does not mean that men should die. But this is inevitable... And no matter how strongly we feel that this technological, capitalistic, democratic establishment must collapse, there is no sign of its happening in the near future. This system is going to flourish, that's obvious. So there's no point harbouring false hopes. We have to find a way out...yes I repeat... suicides are deplorable but—

B: What you are saying is very important! You are so knowledgeable... May I repeat what I just asked you? See, is there no simple solution? There must be... Does no one give this a thought? I mean, has this been thought about at a global level?

A: Look, there's no time for that now. Like you, everybody was moved... And they all asked this same question: Is there an easy solution? [*B wants to ask something.*] No! We don't have the time. Listen. As these people came here, like this, together...

B: But how did so many of them come here together?

A: Hmm! From what I've gathered, they were in a company bus on their way to a picnic. There was a road block because of a farmers' agitation. It's not clear if the driver was drunk, but he rammed the speeding bus into the right side of the road, towards a pit in some agricultural land. The bus crashed. All of them died and came here. As they said all this, Khanduji stood there, listening. The others were jostling against each other, excited, there was total mayhem. I tried to calm them down. Just then this woman arrived—

B: [*Surprised, his voice louder than usual.*] Which woman?

A: That one, sleeping at the back...

B: [*Gets up and moves to the back.*] That one? The other one sleeping behind him is a woman?

A: [*Pulling him back.*] Shh...! Sit here...yes, that's a woman... Godavaribai. She was standing there with the others...

protesting where the bus plunged...into that farmland. The bus ploughed into her...she died...her name is Godavari. She is Khanduji's wife.

B: Oh! That's why they are sleeping together.

A: No. And they're not sleeping together! They're sleeping wherever they can find a place to lie down... [*Pause*] Then everybody quietened down a bit—

B: Oh! I see! It means this woman finally found her way here... I mean a woman here—I mean just like that...amid all these men...a woman.

A: It's not that way... I think we should talk frankly. We are both men so why be shy? Look here, that woman came here, but she's not like the women of our class. She is like Khanduji. Ever since she arrived she hasn't uttered a word. She is absolutely horrible... [*Suddenly irritated*] It's not like that, you see, and...what can you say of such a woman...emancipated...but what can you expect Khanduji's wife to be?

B: Oh, no! That's not what I meant.

A: Then what did you mean? Are we going to deceive one another...you know this guilt... In the end, it's all meaningless. But men die of that, what the fuck. For so many days that's what has been happening...the same thing—

[Temporary pause]

B: I'm sorry... I mean—

[Long pause]

A: Tell me one thing. What part of a woman's body do you fancy the most? Should I guess? Should I? You are just like me. You like breasts, like I do. What a miraculous creation...a marvel of nature. They are the most beautiful thing in the world. Her breasts...the possibility of milk in them...that's what you favour the most, right? [*B is silent.*] Don't be shy. [*Suddenly he raises his voice.*] But this is not true of Godavari's breasts. With such sexual fantasies, at that crucial moment people like us just...anyway. So this is his wife Goda—Godavari. Even when she came here her forehead wasn't adorned with kumkum. That means he obviously died before his wife. That's why she was standing there in protest. She is not too bad...kind of charming in fact. But...her face is so numb...dreary. Just like his. Seeing her, they went kind of insane...excited. Khanduji and Goda stood in a corner. They hadn't even spoken a word to each other. They just stood there. We sat down all over the place. Now and then we would look. [*B too looks at them. This time A does not protest.*] Look...now look. And why're you so restless?

B: No, I'm not.

[He gets up and tries to peer out of his contained space.]

A: Look, look outside as well. That would be even better. You can see what's outside. Spaces just like this, even out there... Look. [*Sharp lights fall on the audience, moving all around.*] Look, just like us, people all queued up, waiting... [*B walks about restlessly.*] Hey, such restlessness is not good... You're waiting? For what?

B: Why aren't we going ahead? What happens next?

A: The same feelings haunted us. Just then my attention was drawn to these two. They were sitting calmly. Then it struck me. I spoke to—you know that financial adviser I spoke of a while ago—I spoke to him first. Then the two of us, once again, explained a few things to the others...

B: What things?

[There's a pause. A doesn't reply immediately. Cautiously he goes near the two sleeping at the back and returns. Then looks at B.]

A: Actually that should be told a little later. We had to linger over it for a long time. So why should it be any different with you?

B: But why waste time? There's nothing as boring as waiting... [*Looking behind*] I don't know how these people can sit about so coolly—

A: How can these people! [*Pause*] You're correct. Let me tell you. You must be put through these stages. Otherwise people like us see the unwanted side at a very inconvenient time. Then a momentary asceticism envelops us!... For once, let there be a purging of all the wrong ideas. Let no unwanted thought come to us at the crucial time. Otherwise we lose the vigour just when we need it. Our friends who were here before us—they didn't have such unwanted thoughts, so they went ahead. And I stayed behind. [*Momentary pause*] Who tried to stop all this from happening? Me! [*Glancing backwards*] Who went out of his way to protect them? Me!... You know, just five minutes after these two arrived, the others immediately got them to do their work—'Lay out the mattresses, fetch water'... I pleaded with them not to do that. But they went ahead, and who remained behind burdened with a feeling of guilt? Me! Fuck, there's no place for the fair-minded in this world... Others do fine...whether it's those from that crowd or these two... [*B gets up and glances about.*] What do you want now? [*B gestures for water.*] Water? Look, it's there...to the left of those two sleeping... No! Don't wake up Goda. Fetch it yourself... Go get yourself a drink, and get one for me too.

[B goes into the dark to get water. There's a pause. A has calmed down.]

A: OK. So you're bored, waiting. And you're surprised that those two are not bored. Even the others were equally surprised. At that time, I once again stood up for those two.

B: And earlier? When did you stand up for them?

A: Oh, come on, didn't I explain the reasons for his committing suicide to the others? Did you know of them before?... And then I tried to stop the others from getting them to do all sorts of work... But let that be. With you, everything will happen quickly. Some things will have to be explained to you. There's no option. Listen... Pay attention. Just as I have been laying out the facts till now, I'm going to continue to show you both sides of everything. For people like us, such subtleties, such intricacies, matter. Now this sensitivity itself gets us into...but that apart...

listen carefully—we are waiting, aren't we? Don't you feel it's the same as the waiting when we were alive?

B: Absolutely.

A: That's the beauty of this place. We remain what we had become. What had become of us when we were alive remains intact. We have got used to waiting for something or the other. Look at it this way: we have got into the habit of waiting for something or the other—what is yet to come, a good future. Once we progress to a certain level, this invariably happens... [*A's face amply exhibits his self-absorbed, pretentious, high moral stand.*] Look at Khanduji...after quite a bit of time, he too became a bit restless. Because he too has entered this new system, this capitalist world, you see. When that happens then... people—that is us—become greedy...see, we must accept it. There's nothing wrong in it. It happens to everyone. It's like this—even as we begin to rejoice at the birth of a new baby, different worries befall us. Can the child hear well? Are his growth parameters correct? Hope he is not retarded? And his memory?... Teach him songs... Which school will admit him?... What about his profession, foreign education, monetary planning...his marriage? Then his children and their problems! And to top it all, what if it is a girl? Hope she will not be assertive, and the 'women's liberation' kind... Take another example. Now if I win a nice case as a lawyer, I won't enjoy this victory in itself... See, I am openly using myself as an example. What happens when I win a case is that I get worried, wondering whether the next case will be better than this one, or if I will get good publicity... See how openly and frankly I am saying all this...but that's the point...we look at everything in an instrumentalist way in this modern world. I have some American friends who worry whether the next Christmas party they are invited to will be better, and they're restless for the whole year. It's as bad as commodity fetishism, the other problem of today. It's the other side of the coin... an avarice beyond one's needs...and then this greed is satiated by somebody, in fact used by somebody. And our participation decreases. Someone else starts controlling our lives—whether it is the advertising world or the corporates or the media...we have become extremely greedy... There's solace even in understanding and accepting it. You feel relaxed for a while, even by that... [*Temporary pause*] Sorry! It's only me who has been talking. I am an extrovert... And to top it, because of all that transpired here... Somehow I need to get over it.

B: No! No, you speak very well. You are absolutely right... any easy solution?

A: Why, are you feeling restless?

B: Yes I am a bit restless—is there no solution?

A: There is... Don't you feel a little comforted knowing this? At that time we felt the same. Later we felt we should become like those two. That was the solution. Do you too feel the same? You feel envious of them, right? One should be able to be like them. Quickly, let's do what we did then. Let's first do some yoga...a bit of shavasana... anulom, vilom...

B: Because of that will we go ahead? It's unbearable here, claustrophobic...what a fucking small place this is—

A: What do you mean by 'a fucking small place'? This is SPACE...call it a space. Pay careful attention to this entire space...then you will realize that after death, space becomes elastic. When all those other people were here, it had become huge, this same space... After they left... [*B grows more restless.*] And as restlessness increases, the space shrinks and time gets stretched...as restlessness increases, the space shrinks even more, and then time is stretched to the extreme... What is space according to Jain philosophy? Space is something that can accommodate things...and time is a thing that accommodates events... According to the Jains...

B: Let your Jains go to hell...how long do we wait—

A: You have to wait here for a while. Still, I am taking you ahead, on the fast track. It took us three to four days to get to the stage of shavasana.

B: Oh, my God! This is killing.

A: Come on, lie down over here. Now do as I tell you. Take a deep breath. [*B is prostrate. A is constantly talking, but it's obvious he's agitated. His words and his actions contradict each other. He walks about restlessly. Occasionally he goes to the back and looks at the two sleeping figures.*] Take another deep breath. Release. Now, without moving a single part of your body, do as I say. Imagine that you're sleeping on the shore of a calm ocean. Now imagine that you're looking at your own body from outside...at your shava...

your corpse. Do as I tell you and concentrate on different parts of your body...now one at a time, relax your toes... now the soles of both the feet...relax your ankle joints... rest your entire weight on the ground—don't burden yourself with anything. Loose...relaxed... Let both the calves loosen up...both the kneecaps...the part below the knees... loosen both the thighs...outer side loose...relaxed...slowly pay attention to the slackened breathing...the inner part of the thighs...the fork between the legs. [*B abruptly jerks his legs, shaking his neck as if in the midst of convulsions.*] Hey, why are you moving? [*B sits upright.*] Huh, you got up? You completed this phase much faster than we did. Your body is now nothing but a corpse—shava and still you can't do shavasana...do you follow anything? Actually our sensitivity increases here...and yours has, much more—

[Pause. B sits upright.]

B: I'm sorry. I'm troubled. What you say is correct. But— [*Pause. Sitting up, B shakes his hands and legs.*] What happens next? Um? Rebirth?

A: No! What are you talking?

B: Then why is this happening only to me? Am I at fault? What is to happen to me?

A: Don't be afraid. The same thing happened to us too. Just that it happened faster in your case...because I am preparing you. Think of this as a preparation for the life ahead, for our future—

B: But I don't seem to be able to handle it.

A: There's nothing wrong with that. There's another side to it, as I said earlier. Every time I will present the other side of the story. We people are like that. We probe deep... into subtleties...sensitively. You know why it is happening like this? Because, basically, there's nothing wrong about such a thing happening to us. See, this society has regressed because we are satisfied with the little we have...there's no positive attitude. We've stopped being proactive. We must look to the future...what's wrong with that? Um? Consumerism and commodification, it's fine mouthing such big words, but basically what is wrong in wanting a better life? Um? And then these things, anyway, are beyond us...we are not to be held responsible. That man progressed and came this far, is that our fault? There are problems at every stage. In the earlier days, people died of influenza and malaria—what was the life expectancy then?... Haven't we progressed? It's bound to be like this... What is the harm in being ambitious? And what's wrong with being restless because of that?

B: You're right! If everyone thinks of his own good, eventually everybody will benefit. One should think only of how good things will come your way—then automatically—

A: [*Suddenly annoyed*] Oh no, it's not that way. That's not what I meant to say. What you're saying is all wrong—it doesn't happen that way, that's been proved beyond doubt. What I'm saying is deeper, more subtle...try to understand. You're saying what that bald, fair, sloppy man from the other group said, condemning Khanduji. We had a fight, with Khanduji and I on one side and the rest on the other... And in spite of all of this, if one of them asked for anything, Khanduji would promptly comply...I tell you it's just this way with such people, but that apart... What I'm saying is entirely different. You said that one should only think for oneself, that is not what I'm saying...it is such an escapist logic. How can you say such a thing?... You are all scoundrels—

[Abruptly A stops. B is astounded. After a while, unable to bear it, B speaks. He is irritated.]

B: What do you mean? Huh? You can't yell at me like this... I am not a nonentity like those two friends of yours—like that Khandu, and that Godavari or Narmada, whatever she is called... Defended them? You defended them? Then what should I do? Because I am stuck with you here, you... It's only because you have been here from the start that I'm listening to you. Now I feel you're manipulating me. You have a hidden agenda. You're not as saintly as you claim to be.

A: I'm sorry. I'm not saintly. I'm a simple man, you see—

B: Now look here, stop talking from every side. Anyway it's getting unbearable, waiting here so long. If I could have gone outside, I wouldn't have waited here even a minute.

[Pause]

A: Please listen to me. Now I'm feeling even guiltier. Believe me, I am doing all this for our own good... It was fine till now. What will happen here after this is even more—

B: What is going to happen here? You keep harping on that.

A: Just look around you. Like in an apartment in a city, you can look into the neighbouring apartments here too. Don't you see the same scene all around you? As if all the walls are of glass. Look, there are numerous spaces all over, just like ours, as far as the eye can see. [*Here the harsh lights are on the audience.*] Look there to your left. A while ago there was a big group, remember?

B: Yes. You're right.

A: It went ahead...and that girl there, who was all alone sometime back? A sweet, adolescent girl of sixteen—you remember, you were ogling at her? She too left. Now some others have replaced her. That...that old man there—[*Indicates with a wave that he too has left.*]... In the last ten minutes—I mean from the time we started doing the shavasana, half the people around us have been replaced—

B: That's right. But where did they go?

A: Where? They went ahead...further. After having gone through the chaos, the restlessness, they went ahead... See, there are numerous spaces—see how many people there are—between them and us, do you feel any difference?

B: Yes. I feel it...we are relatively calm...they are more restless. They are desperately in wait—

A: Correct—they are moving about in tortuous circles, glancing at their wrist-watches...pulling at their hair... thrashing each other...once it becomes uncontrollable... moving ahead. [*Looking at him.*] But we are still stuck...

people are trooping in...getting restless...when sufficiently restless, they move ahead...if you keep looking, it gets maddening...and a frightening feeling takes over. It is just we, alone, who are stuck. The rest are moving ahead. We alone are stranded. The rest are going ahead. Stuck alone, the rest all—

[B is extremely restless. A is also in the same condition.]

B: I can't stand still like this any longer.

A: That's good!

B: Good?

A: Yes, that means now you have a chance to move ahead.

[B feels a bit elated. Pause. B paces. Both look outside.]

B: My hands seem to be twisting—

A: I know.

B: I mean they are twisting but not hurting... Twisting—

A: In medical jargon, it is called a state of Extreme Muscular Discomfort.

B: You're right. It's extreme...muscular...discomfort. Why are we waiting?... Oh, my legs and my back, even they are twisting. That's the worst.

A: This is what happened to us. The body turns about grotesquely...it is uncontrollable...like squirming out of an unbearable sexual urge...wriggling, writhing, insatiable, ravenous...and that's just the beginning. And do you know what one of them thought of? He was thin—short guy with thick soda glasses...seemed like an accountant. He had a runny nose. You know what came to his mind? He thought he would get relief if someone gave him a vigorous massage. Then all of them got a massage from Khanduji and Godavari.

[B looks back at the two. Moves in their direction.]

A: [*Loudly*] Please don't wake them up. It was wrong on my part to have told you everything... Please, please control your twisting body and listen. I need you, we need each other. If they get up and if we keep looking at them, a feeling of camaraderie will develop between sensitive people like us and them. What we are expected to do later gets delayed...then we get left behind—look what happened to me. I have observed all these spaces, studied everything carefully. People like my erstwhile friends move ahead, and millions like Khanduji and Godavari are left stranded. In fact, they are the ones in the majority. But they are not easily visible...they simply merge...just like that...into the darkness! They do not shine, you see. But basically they don't experience this restlessness, so they don't see it as a problem. But we can't be like them. So we don't belong to either group...then where do we stand?

B: Now you are speaking against them—

A: [*Shouts*] No! You're stupid!

B: You're yelling again. I can shout too.

A: Look, I've spent a lot of time here. It's maddening. I tell you, even when the others got their massage, I stood firmly in support of these two. I tried to get away from the others, sit near these two. It's not easy. People like us can't manage it. I've spent a lot of time here and you've just—

B: Shut up—

A: Listen to me. It took us a lot of time to see the solution. Actually it's not out of this world. It has always existed... we always knew it but it was at the back of our minds... now we have to put it into practice. I'll tell you what happened, it'll save time.

B: You're manipulating me—keep quiet. I'm not going to listen to you.

> *[A tries to say something. Then keeps quiet. He clutches the chair firmly till his face reddens. He sits stiffly, unmoving, suppressing his restlessness. B's restlessness increases. He is staring outside.]*

B: [*At his wits' end*] Hey, all of them keep going ahead... that old lady who was there a while ago, even she can't be seen...and all them over there—

> *[A is quiet. B looks at him angrily, but A remains quiet. B gets even more restless.]*

B: [*Again looking outside, bellows*] Look, look! If this continues, only people like these two will remain behind. And the two of us in their crowd! Even that long-nosed, beggar-like person who had been waiting so long has left... Say something...I beg you...I apologize...I am at fault. I don't want to get left behind. Please...tell me why it's happening this way? Why is it that only the two of us are left behind?

A: I'll tell you, but don't interrupt. Even speaking coherently is getting strenuous. I can't concentrate any more. If I wait another ten minutes, I'm not sure what will happen. Maybe I will beat you up...clobber you. Even if we are dead, our bodies still exist. Remember we're able to feel pain even now... If it gets unbearable I will gouge your eyes out...I—

B: Talk, please! Don't stop now... I'll agree with everything you say.

A: [*In a restrained but chilling voice, like a cold fire, trying to be matter of fact, but also trying to influence and manipulate B with the sheer horror of the narrative.*] The same thing happened to us. Then we realized that the people moving ahead—the ones released from here—mostly moved ahead as a group from a specific area. The entire group would be restless, then move ahead. We realized that Khanduji and Goda were still calm, never restless. And till this restlessness was felt by everyone, we would be stranded. Everybody had to be restless, or we had to find an alternative so only those who were restless could go ahead. Some of the group asked these two to be restless. They couldn't manage that. One of them—the economist I spoke of—he tried explaining it to them. No change... No! Don't you go near them. All our efforts were exhausted. One smart youngster tried coaxing them with a description of all the goodies they could get ahead, as if he was running a marketing campaign...assured them that if they became restless they would go to heaven next... Khanduji was partly carried away by this...I noticed his hands curling up. But Godavari was numb—a cold glob. It was also difficult for Khanduji to be restless for too long.

Then someone abused them, slapped them, and much more. Still it was difficult for them to make them restless... Goda, the poor thing, she was trying, her sari pallu fell off her withered breasts...they harassed her to the extreme... but all in vain...

[There is an uncomfortable silence. B attempts to say something. A gestures that he should remain silent.]

Our bodies throbbed, just like yours is now. We hit our hands and legs against the walls and the floor. I was convinced we would begin to thrash one another... No one could contain their anger at these two. In the end—do you remember that bald, fair, fat guy I spoke of? He dragged Godavari onto the floor. That long-nosed person pushed Khandu to one side. The others encircled the two. I spoke up, but the two of them held me back. That fatso ripped Godavari's torn sari, stripped her of her undergarments. Lowering his trousers, he fell on her. I freed myself, turned away. I could hear the sounds—of struggling, of the fat man and the others grunting. Goda made no sound... That fat man raped her.

Fatso got up and sat across from me. The thudding of his body gradually eased off. His face was still contorted into grotesque expressions. But his face also showed a sense of confidence about the future. There was no worry. Every breath of his was confident. [*Pause*]

He said to me in a husky voice, 'Now you do it...don't think twice...that's the only way. Let's see if at least this will make the bitch restless... Let's see if she can crave for the future... How can she not long for a better future? The future can't be worse than this...it can only get better. At least now she will want, crave... Let's see...this fucking breed of women...and whatever happens...I'm already feeling good. I have this gut feeling...my work will get done... now it's your turn...go.' I yelled at the fatso. I called him a motherfucker...he just laughed.

Hearing my shout, the others stood frozen. I felt a little better but the restlessness was intense. Fatso sat there, looking at us. His body grew steady, but his face continued to twitch. He was now laughing with self-confidence.

Nobody knew what exactly to do next.

Suddenly, something charged in from the darkness on the left. It wasn't clear if it was a man or something else. It looked like a human, but it was pellucid, translucent. The creature went up close to the fatso and muttered something in his ear...then immediately disappeared into the darkness.

Remember I told you there was a short, thin guy with thick soda glasses? He was the first one to gather his courage and approach the fatso. The fat man with the twitching face lay prostrate. Despite the twitch on his face, it looked carefree, completely satisfied. He looked at the bespectacled man silently, his hands raised as if blessing him, then ordered him to go to Godavari. The bespectacled man went to her. The others encircled them once again. The sounds of scuffling were heard once again, but less grunting this time. And this time, a momentary moaning sound from Khanduji... The bespectacled man raped Godavari.

He, too, became calm and his face began to twitch. Looking at this, the financial advisor moved forward with determination. I couldn't bear it anymore. I had spoken at length with him. I had found him far more sensible than the others. I moved, stood between him and Goda. I didn't utter a word. He said, 'See, we are dead. These bodies of ours are not real... In fact, if these two cooperate like we did, this illusory body you seem to have—this maya—even that won't remain... Even this rape is illusory...all you see is unreal... Look at the fatso, then these two... See, they should actually join hands with us. But instead they...try to understand. I mean it's they who are responsible for this whole goddamn thing.'

I was dazed. I didn't even register his going past me. When I came to my senses, he was pushing Godavari, who lay groaning on her side, onto her back. He spread her legs, bent forward and lay on her.

There was no sound this time. I looked away. After a while, that intellectual, that economist and financial advisor came to me and said it was my turn.

I shook my head in denial.

He raised his fist but the fatso pulled him away.

In twos and threes they went to the back and did the same thing. Now that youngster. Then the one with the big nose...the others pushed and dragged him to Godavari. They removed his trousers and pushed him on top of her.

[Pause]

Once they were all done, they lay on their backs, writhing and moaning. If you ask me, that long-nosed youngster was not able to rape Godavari. I'm sure of that. I think that's also true of a few others. But all of them acted as if they had done it.

Then they sat up and waited. Only the fatso still lay on the floor. The others didn't have to wait for long. The apparition of the man-creature reappeared. He whispered something in each one's ear, even the ear of the long-nosed youngster, the one who feigned the rape. They quietened, rolled about, their faces twitching, laughing now and then.

I turned. Godavari lay motionless. Khanduji was restless. But he couldn't do a thing. There was not a single sound from him...

Crouching in a corner, my head tucked between my knees, I sat, clasping my twisting hands and legs. I wept bitterly... pitying myself. Only I remained restless. It was unbearable. The loneliness was eating me up. Then I decided I too should rape her. I too wanted to meet that illusory man. I became aroused, looked at them. Khanduji and Godavari sat silent as before. I looked at the others for support, but to my horror the entire lot had disappeared! I got a terrible shock. I stood up with difficulty and went towards Khanduji. I shouted, 'Where are the rest?! Where have they gone?'

He sat dumb, the motherfucker. I charged at Goda. She... whether she was sleeping or unconscious, God alone knows. I had to rape her without any support... They'd all left...

those bastards. They should be shot...only I remained. Alone! As I bent to straighten Goda, I heard a tiny sound from Khanduji. I looked up, startled. Khanduji hadn't moved, but suddenly I was shit scared. I hated myself. I tried, but... Try to understand... It's difficult for me to say this... You see, I was left alone...without help. I didn't have even the courage to pretend to rape like that youngster. I accept this.

I turned away, terribly upset with myself. I slapped myself till I bled...how could I have so little courage? I hit my head against the floor, right here at this spot. Khanduji just sat there, numb.

[There is an extremely uncomfortable pause. A is again sitting, tightly clutching his hands and legs. B, highly agitated, writhes. That B is not yet ready to commit the rape is obvious. He attempts to say something to that effect. But A stops him with a wave of his hand and continues to talk.]

I realized it fully. I would need help...I am not impotent, but I need help... I need help to commit the rape... This is a fact and I have to accept it. I know you too will need help...we are sensitive people. I knew this the moment I saw you! See, it's nothing to feel ashamed of... It was easy for the group because they knew each other, you see—

No, don't speak...I know we're horrible...that's a given fact... What now...what do we do about it? What he said earlier was so true. These aren't our real bodies...and these two are the ones really responsible—shit, why should we suffer? They have to be rammed... I mean we have to act. We can't sit about passively...

And look here...you can confess at the end. Just accept the whole thing and forget it...that's what I've been doing all this while after you came. Now I am drained... It's catharsis—but somewhere down the road you have to participate in the actual act... And such an opportunity is rare. There will be many occasions to confess later—that's invariable...it's always there for people like us...please trust me...[*A momentarily pauses. B is still in two minds, petrified.*]

Look here, are you getting unbearably restless or not? It's not happening to them. Let me repeat: they're responsible—finished. There's only one way out...rape... That's it! Like I said earlier, we are always doing it anyway. Always raping, always using our might to exploit somebody. But the systems are such that it goes unnoticed. The only difference here is that it is bare, visible to all. At one stage of progress this happens. History proves it... Your hands and legs are twitching, aren't they? Now is the point of no return. You're addicted to it...

[*B is still flabbergasted. A abruptly changes his stance, and assumes an aggressive tone.*] Do you wish to become like them and stay here? If you're committed, you can become like them. There is a need for people like them. Otherwise who will we rape? Would you like to become like them?

[*B takes a few steps forward, stops. A is aware that he can control B. This makes him even more impatient.*]

But like I said, it's your choice... Nobody can force you... This is a democracy... You may stay here with them if you wish... But at least help me...please. I'm not asking for much. She is completely bedraggled. How can she resist? But even on such a bedraggled...I mean, it's tough! Spread her legs like this...here... [*B goes towards them. A sees this.*] Good! Come...come quickly.

[B stumbles towards A. A pulls him up. Both stand there nervously in a moment of silence. Then holding hands, they move, roll Godavari onto her back. Suddenly it is pitch dark. The continuous, deep, moaning sound of a woman can be heard. When the lights come on, A and B are no longer on stage. They have gone ahead. Goda and Khandu are lying in a dishevelled state. Goda's torn sari is spread out in the front.]

CROSSROADS

Translated from the original Marathi play *Chowk*
by Shanta Gokhale

[Several characters move about the stage making a variety of wordless gestures. Some appear highly agitated; others are calmer either because they are unaffected or afraid. If a fight breaks out among the agitated lot, the calm ones standing beside them might only protect themselves, but will continue to remain calm.

In the midst of this chaos, Achyut Athavale, a man of about 65 or 70, walks from one end of the stage to the other. He too is calm, but the quality of his calmness is different from the others'. The sutradhar[1] *intercepts him as he is leaving the stage.]*

SUTRADHAR: Sir, Athavale Sir, just a minute.

ACHYUT: Oh it's you!

SUTRADHAR: Yes, it's me. The sutradhar.

---

1. Traditionally Sanskrit plays used to start with a sequence between the SUTRADHAR—the narrator/manager / director/ co-ordinator or one may call him a 'conductor'—of the play and the NATI—the lead female actor. She is supposed to be his wife or lover. She is normally late and he urges her to come and start the play. She arrives. They introduce the audience to the subject of the play and then the play starts. This convention was inherited by early Marathi plays though it has not been used for many years now. This play uses the convention in a modified way—for one, it has no Nati (There is an explanation for her absence given by the Sutradhar) and it uses the Sutradhar also as a 'one man chorus' who ends up taking an active part in the play at the end.

ACHYUT: So where's your Nati? Isn't there a convention…

SUTRADHAR: Sir, we needed five female actors but managed to get only four. One of them was supposed to be the sutradhar—I mean breaking the covention, our sutradhar was supposed to be female. We tried very hard, but nothing worked. We had to change everything around. You'll say these are extra-artistic excuses…

ACHYUT: Not at all. Things are complicated. I know. Theatre, art, they are complex transactions. And to get female actors…very difficult. But let me not keep you… sorry…

SUTRADHAR: Please sir. You are saying some very interesting things. But there's so much noise around I can hardly hear you. [*Signals to the actors to lower their voices.*] Not much of an audience, but they are here and they have settled down. I might as well start the play. You're giving a lecture today aren't you? What's your subject, Sir?

ACHYUT: 'The Polarization of Identities and Marathi Poetry'.

SUTRADHAR: Sounds great. I'd love to be there. But I must start the play now. You will of course give your—

ACHYUT: No need to…I'm with you. Don't worry. Shall I carry on?

[The sutradhar waves him on. Achyut exits. He halts on the way to pick up a ragged book, glances at it momentarily and leaves. The other actors' voices and gestures grow louder. The sutradhar casts a glance over them.]

SUTRADHAR: That was Achyut Athavale. Achyut Athavale! Hell! I thought people would recognize him at least, if not me. [*Shrugs*] Well, I guess I'll have to tell you who he is. Briefly. My friend, philosopher, guide... everything. Also a character in the play. Both identities will be present here, together. I mean he'll be my friend, philosopher, guide etc. That's one identity. And he'll be a character in the play. That's the other identity. He's an economist, an intellectual. His interests range with ease from literature to philosophy. [*Pauses*] He has his opinions of course; but is also extraordinarily tolerant of other peoples' opinions. Which means he is one of those people whom some other people see as causing confusion. He's involved with many social movements...but enough of that for the moment. Every person is a mesh of different identities. And some of these identities arise out of mutually unconnected frameworks. I'm not going to introduce you to all the identities of all these characters right at the beginning of the play...I'll stick to one identity each. [*Turns around. Seeks out Pratap from the crowd. Pratap is 35 to 40 years old, middle class, paunchy. He carries a newspaper and is dressed in a nondescript pair of trousers and shirt. The sutradhar leads him to the front. Pratap pays no heed to him. He continues what he is doing.*] Let's take his identity. He is one of those whose emotions are quickly aroused. It's easy to see that this man is one of those whose emotions are quickly aroused—inflamed you may say. Of course, prevailing circumstances are conducive for that to happen. But even with that, his emotions are particularly quickly aroused. He's a troubled man. They are all like that...the people on this side [*By now two sub-groups have formed on the stage, somewhat together but still apart. They continue with their movements and gestures*]...people whose emotions are quickly aroused. [*One person beats up another, preferably a man hits a woman. The others in the group split and stand confronting one another with aggressive gestures. Those belonging to the calm group remain totally calm in spite of their proximity to the commotion nearby]* And the emotions of these people here [*indicating the calm group*] are never aroused. Let me explain. There's this lot whose emotions are very quickly aroused. Say a leaf falls off a tree on their heads...and bang! Their emotions are aroused. In fact, their emotions are already in an aroused state. It is easy for those whose identity is of people whose emotions are quickly aroused to come together, that's all. Now these others... Nothing that happens ever arouses their emotions. A woman is raped before their eyes, or Babri Masjid is demolished, or Sikhs are killed in a pogrom, or bombs explode...nothing. Then what does one expect when they encounter everyday events of some importance... You can see that can't you, just by looking at them?

Anyway [*bringing Pratap to the front*], this is Pratap. Pratap Chavan, one of those whose emotions are quickly aroused. He possesses other identities too. For instance, he's a male, a Hindu, one of the very few people today who still respects intellectuals like Achyut. He's a family man. Caste—Kunbi Maratha. He's done a diploma in mechanical engineering from some third-rate college and a small course in software engineering. So these are also his identities. He's Achyut's neighbour. These days he's inclined to love America because America seems to be inclining towards an anti-Pakistan position. He lost his job yesterday, the fourth in three years, for no fault of his— [*Even as he speaks, Pratap flies into a rage. He shouts and flings his footwear and other things around. Nobody comes to his help. He exits. The activity at the back continues for a while. The sutradhar watches, stunned. Then somebody's foot touches somebody else's foot. Those whose emotions are quickly aroused begin to riot. Some others run away. Some lie down pretending to be dead. The rioters leave. The riot has lasted only a few seconds but the effect has been chilling. Peace reigns now. Everybody exits. The sutradhar begins to speak. Within a few seconds, it gets noisy again at the back. The characters arrange the stage to represent a traffic jam. In short, after a few minutes of peace, we're back to city noise and activity. The sutradhar continues to speak.*]

What I'd like to explain is, this play is the product of a certain process. You saw Pratap, right? Pratap Chavan who lost his job? Well, sometime ago, he and Achyut Athavale were travelling by bus. It so happened that I was sitting behind them that day. Achyut Athavale, as we heard earlier, was on his way to give a lecture. Pratap Chavan had time on his hands since he had lost his job the previous day. He still hadn't told even his wife and children that he had lost his job. His emotions were aroused as it is; and anyway, there was nothing special about losing a job. [*Four characters get into a bus at the back—Achyut, Pratap, Pushpatai and*

Honap. Pushpatai is about 35, attractive, always apprehensive. Honap is around 45; a government employee, sweaty, stout, with carefully parted hair and a glutinous smile.]

That day Pratap had nothing to do. He needed to engage his mind in something. So he set off with Achyut to hear him speak. In fact, he had made a habit of it over the last few years. Each time he lost a job, he would go with Achyut to hear him speak. Achyut spoke on big issues, like social, political and economic problems. It calmed Pratap to hear him.

But that day his emotions were aroused. I feel quite scared when I look at him. And concerned too. I can't help being sympathetic towards him, as I am to all of us here. My heart goes out to him. My heart goes out to all of us. This is the grey area of our times. It's like this. At one moment someone is in the group of people whose emotions are quickly aroused. The next minute he's joined the group whose emotions are not quickly aroused. So you can't see things in black and white. You have to sympathize with everybody. [*Pause*] And those times when you are fucking angry with everybody, you feel no sympathy for anybody. It was that kind of strange situation on this particular day. Nothing unusual. [*Suddenly people run onto the stage and riot. Some fight with sticks, some throw stones and some run away screaming. The riot lasts only a few moments, but it shakes you. When the rioters exit, footwear is scattered everywhere. People in the bus who have stood up in fear, sit down.*]

All in all, we live in the gaps between riots or the time between two sets of aroused emotions. That's when we are not part of them. So, on that day too, one riot had just ended. Or rather had been ended. For one of the four or five normal reasons. A few passengers still remained in the bus. Let's get to know them—an opinion pollster's sample. We already know Achyut and Pratap. To make our sample scientific, we need a woman. Let's ask this one. [*Approaching a woman in the bus.*] May we know a little about you please? Very briefly. Give us just a couple of your identities. We have an intelligent audience. They'll get the rest.

PUSHPATAI: Oh? Okay. I...I am Pushpatai Gogate. Brahmin. Most residents of our society are Brahmins. That's one thing my husband did before he...

SUTRADHAR: You mean your husband...?

PUSHPATAI: He died a year-and-a-half ago.

SUTRADHAR: So then you are...

PUSHPATAI: Yes. Alone. Earlier too I used to manage everything. Along with my job. [*To herself*] Now it's a little risky. Even if you keep your mangalsutra on, society residents do come to know. It's a Brahmin society but even then...[*Aloud*] The name of the society is Gurukrupa.

SUTRADHAR: [*Turning to the man beside her*] And may we know something about you?

HONAP: I'm her neighbour. I accompany her home every day. She's alone, see?

SUTRADHAR: Yes, I see. But your name and all that?

HONAP: Honap. From Gurukrupa Society. A Brahmin of course. I'm an OS in ZP. Permanent. Nobody gives any importance to Brahmins these days in government jobs. But I'm permanent. My office is next to hers.

PUSHPATAI: [*Interrupting*] There's another thing about me. I love bhavgeets.[2]

HONAP: So do I. Very much.

SUTRADHAR: [*Addressing Pushpatai*] Pushpatai, what do you have to say about the riot that happened a little while ago? It started near your office.

PUSHPATAI: I...I don't want to say anything.

SUTRADHAR: But...

PUSHPATAI: I said I don't want to talk. I didn't see a thing. Please don't discuss this with me.

SUTRADHAR: [*To Honap*] Your opinion...about the riot?

HONAP: See, those who want to die, die. On top of that they have a grouse against government servants like me. We are supposed to be corrupt. Although we are part of a society that is corrupt through and through, we are the ones who must bear the brunt. They set fire to three buses the last time. Government property. But the bastards think they own it.

---

2. Kind of light (read mushy) songs in Marathi—mostly about love and romance. They are quite popular.

SUTRADHAR: [*Turning towards Pratap*] Your opinion, Mr Chavan?

PRATAP: Riots can't be avoided. Those who are...in the sense the people behind them remain untouched. Who were the people who died? Ours or theirs?

SUTRADHAR: In this riot it wasn't very clear who our people were.

PUSHPATAI: [*Cuts in*] To hell with that. [*Pause*] Which people lose jobs? We. [*Pause. Shouts*] Riots? Let them fucking happen.

SUTRADHAR: [*Quickly moves the mike away and holds it before Achyut.*] What about you Sir?

ACHYUT: Er...umm can't tell you in one sentence. People will listen to a whole speech and pick one line out of it and twist... No, no. I won't give an opinion casually, like this. We can meet later. I would love to talk about it.

[He is obviously a little upset. Pause]

SUTRADHAR: [*Sits down in his own place in the bus.*] So that's how the bus was moving, stopping and starting, all the way through the area where the riot had happened.

[Pause]

ACHYUT: [*To himself*] The whole social texture has changed. Is changing by the day. Can't fathom it. And it's very disturbing at my age. These days, riots end as soon as they have begun. A quick thought...it's because the numbers have decreased in every group of people whose emotions are quickly aroused, who were once held together in a kind of common denominator way by a shared identity. These groups split. As a result, the number of groups has increased. Every issue, -ism or caste produces ten groups. Naturally the number of members subscribing to each one gets smaller. Which means riots don't last long; which in turn means the number of riots increases. It's like little stabs of pain in the stomach instead of one long ache. [*Achyut's voice grows small. Pushpatai looks deeply sad and hums a popular bhavgeet about playing house-house with toy pots and pans. Honap casts a glance of sympathy towards her and inches closer. Pushpatai draws herself in. Cutting Achyut, the sutradhar comes forward.*]

SUTRADHAR: So Achyut sat looking into space and pondering. Pushpatai Gogate was trying to move as far away from Honap as she could. Achyut was also trying to move away from Pratap, causing him to misinterpret the reason. Achyut thought he himself would have liked to be left alone, to be given some space, had he lost his job. That's why he had moved away, fixed his eyes elsewhere and was consciously not talking to him. Pratap misunderstood him totally. He couldn't understand Achyut at all. He simply couldn't connect the dots.

PRATAP: [*To himself*] Okay. Don't talk to me. Bastards. But Achyut Athavale? How could he? Why?

SUTRADHAR: Pratap was getting more and more agitated. In contrast, there was less agitation on the street. The evening traffic was becoming dense. The speed of the bus was decreasing by the second. The riot had lost steam. The bus was crawling.

[The sutradhar moves towards his seat. On the way he becomes the bus conductor. Both Pushpatai and Honap reach for their money when they see him. Honap stops Pushpatai, coming between her and the conductor.]

PUSHPATAI: [*To Honap*] Please, why do you pay for me every day? It's been two weeks now. [*To herself*] Why not? Fourteen rupees saved. That's four days worth of vegetables. But this is going to cost me. [*Aloud*] You're not going to do it today. I'll pay for myself. Or even for both...

HONAP: Please let it be. What difference does it make whether you buy your ticket or I? We're neighbours after all.

[The sutradhar-conductor returns to his seat.]

PUSHPATAI: This really bothers me a lot.

HONAP: [*Merely smiles. To himself*] Bothers you? Good. Let it. Let it. She never actually stops me. Just talk. Her husband didn't give her what she...

PUSHPATAI: [*To herself*] Neighbour my foot. It's getting a little too much now. Takes bribes, the lout. Let him pay. It's bribe money going. God is watching. But he's getting too fresh. Travels in the same bus, the SOB. What a garish shirt!

[Pushpatai turns away to look outside.]

SUTRADHAR: [*From his seat*] I could see...you can too... that Pratap's grief at losing his job was turning into anger.

The question as always was: who to be angry with? In the old days you knew your enemy. Now you know some, but some remain faceless. The bus is late. Who's the enemy? America and Iraq are at war. Petrol prices shoot up. The Indian economy is impacted. The poor suffer more. Who is the enemy? When Pratap was appointed in this job, he gave a written undertaking that he would not take any leave in the first four months of joining. Riding home four days ago, his scooter bumped over a pothole, he fell off and hurt his bum badly. Which contractor made the road? The bribed councilor...

PRATAP: [*To himself*] Bloody bastard...all of them... fucking bastards...

SUTRADHAR: That meant three days of leave. Yesterday he lost his job. Not his fault. [*Pause*] He couldn't curse the factory either. Not that he even remembered which factory to curse, he'd been thrown out of so many in the last few years.

PRATAP: Ff...ff...ff...ff!

SUTRADHAR: Who is he to get angry with? That's the question bugging Pratap. When something happens repeatedly, it really gets to you. It got to Pratap and he began weeping. The tears just wouldn't stop. Then he remembered Achyut Athavale. He conveniently remembered what Achyut had said in his last lecture in favour of the new labour policy—the hire and fire clause. He was filled with rage. And he lost his temper with confidence.

PRATAP: [*Shouts in the midst of his tears*] Athavale... Mister...Mister Athavale...[*The passengers are startled.*]

SUTRADHAR: How that startled everybody in the bus! Pratap glanced around. The entire busload was looking at him. Seven of them were weeping.

ACHYUT: [*To himself*] Pratap must have felt good to have seven others in the bus weeping with him. It is always comforting to share an identity. No fun being alone. It must have given him confidence.

PRATAP: [*To himself*] Cry you buggers, all of you, cry.

ACHYUT: [*To himself*] But on the other hand he must have felt saddened at losing his unique identity. Everybody was unhappy. Nothing special about him. That must have frustrated him. Tch tch...what now...

[Long pause]

SUTRADHAR: I began to see all these people...Achyut, Pratap, Pushpatai, Honap...people who exchanged a few remarks with each other. But then I began to hear what they were saying to themselves...monologues...the way you can. I'd hear just the conversations or sometimes just the monologues, or sometimes both. I might hear just one spoken thing and nine unspoken things. Even in the old days people said nine things to themselves. But society was a little more homogeneous then. So people would guess each other's nine unspoken thoughts even if they couldn't hear them. You heard even what your enemy was thinking. Like daughters-in-law and mothers-in-law, Dalits and Brahmins, capitalists and communists. There was much that they shared. And now? Now even enemies say the same thing. The Rashtriya Swayanksevak Sangh affiliates and the communists both chant 'Swadeshi', 'Swadeshi'. Both speak against Valentine's Day. But they mean something altogether different! Neither understands the other's unspoken thoughts. Those thoughts come from a totally different place. As with these seven weeping people.

PUSHPATAI: [*To herself*] How loudly he shouted! He's a manly man. Nobody's bothering him. Why is he shouting? And crying? It's scary. Really scary. These people are capable of doing anything at all.

[She too begins to weep quietly, looking out of the window.]

PRATAP: Mister Athavale, I've just remembered. I've lost my job because of people like you.

ACHYUT: Me?

PRATAP: Yes you... You people put all sorts of ideas into the government's head.

ACHYUT: I do?

PRATAP: Yes. I heard what you said in your last lecture. You are...err...a what-you-may-call-it of the new...liberal economy. You support the new labour policy. I heard you say that with my ears...you want a new labour policy based on 'hire and fire'...

ACHYUT: That is quite true

PRATAP: How can both the things be...

ACHYUT: It's a position on a very large, complex issue. You had no business losing your job. The two things are diff...

PRATAP: But in that lecture you were speaking in favour of the other side.

ACHYUT:I still do.

PRATAP: What?

ACHYUT: Dear man, leave alone being able to say what that means in brief, even a whole lecture isn't enough these days. What did I say in my article in *Loksatta* yesterday? That this policy is necessary. But only if the government creates safety nets. If you read everything I write in...*Sakal*, *Loksatta*, *Maharashtra Times*...then you will understand the overall perspective...and the part of my position which you are unhappy with is only a cog in the wheel and in that capacity, it—I must insist—that it is absolutely correct...

PRATAP: What does that do? Eh? What does it do?

[Short pause as Achyut does not understand what Paratap is trying to say.]

ACHYUT: Do? Who's done what to whom?

PRATAP: What does it do to you? What do things ever do to you? [*Pause. To himself*] But I suppose he's right. I did agree with what he said that time... But how the old man changes his stripes!

ACHYUT: [*To himself*] I don't want to show him up as a fool. Damn. Why did he have to lose his job.

PRATAP: [*Paces about in the bus. Very upset. To himself*] I am fed up with this man. I'm mad at him. I'm going to teach the bastard such a lesson one of these days!

[Pause]

SUTRADHAR: And so Pratap and Achyut stopped talking in the middle of their conversation. I couldn't even hear their monologues, they became so monotonous. My ears turned to Pushpatai.

PUSHPATAI: [*Looks back for a second. To herself*] Thank heavens they've stopped talking. Was that talking or fighting? Who could they be? Union men? Communists? I don't like communists. My husband was so against Russia...

HONAP: [*To himself*] They must be economy opening up types, liberals...the bastards. Must be on the side of privatization. Bloody Private types. I had hoped at least this fellow would give the old man an earful. But he clammed up. They've got their knives out for government servants, bastards. Everything should be handed over to the communists.

PUSHPATAI: [*To herself*] The bus is crawling. I'm going to be late again. When's this going to end?

[The bus jolts to a stop. While the sutradhar is saying the following lines, a number of people enter and sit around on the stage. There is confusion. Traffic jam sounds fill the air. By the time things quieten down, four people have sat in a rickshaw in the left-hand corner, two on a scooter between the rickshaw and bus,

and to the extreme right of the bus is a luxury car in which is seated a wealthy couple in their thirties.]

SUTRADHAR: Just then, the bus got caught in a traffic snarl in a square. It came to a dead halt. A riot had just happened. The October heat was deadly. And this traffic jam on top of it. It is said that you can tell a baby's future in the cradle. Similarly, you can tell a traffic jam's future by its beginning. The experienced know which baby is going to grow into an important person. The experienced like us know which jam is going to last long. We knew this jam was one of them.

PUSHPATAI: Oh no! We're stuck.

HONAP: [*Happily*] We're stuck.

PUSHPATAI: [*To herself*] More delay. The exam is on us. How will the children finish their work? Raunak must be hungry. Sayli is no use. She's 13. At that age I was cooking. This one can't put butter on bread for her brother.

HONAP: [*To himself*] I will escort her home again today.

PUSHPATAI: [*To herself*] Ask her to do something and she flies at you, the hussy. Don't discriminate between me and him she says. Who does she think is going to take care of me when I'm old? She? Always busy dolling up. It'll be a blessing if she marries and goes away. Why doesn't Raunak like studying? He's eleven-and-a-half now... And...and... Oh, my God, I am going to miss *Avantika*, my favourite soap on TV... It was going to be revealed in today's episode if her husband's going to walk out on her...

And I am going to miss it!... Hell... Go die. Die. [*She says the last word aloud.*]

HONAP: What's the matter? Don't worry please. I'll see you home. [*Both grow still.*]

PRATAP: [*To himself*] Stuck... The heat's killing... Damn. What's happening? What's holding us? [*He alights from the bus to see.*]

SUTRADHAR: I'll get off to see where he is going in this jam. It'll help me too. I can see lots of people out there. They could be my characters. Caught in the jam. Pratap...

> *[The sutradhar has alighted from the bus. He sees the luxury car with Yash and Supriya in it. There's Patil and Tamhane on a scooter, and Seemantini, Durga and a craftsman from Orissa in a rickshaw with the driver. There is a Warkari*[3] *in one corner, and Pratap. Once the scene is established, the focus will shift from one group to another. The remaining characters will crowd around the group in focus, carrying on with their own business, occasionally acknowledging one another. The sutradhar first approaches Yash and Supriya. Yash is 35, suave, dressed in high-end clothes. Supriya is around 30, beautiful, beautifully formed, slender or almost thin, well-dressed. The Warkari is standing just*

3. Warkari is a popular sect in Maharashtra, well-known for its belief in equality and tolerance. It has been in existence for more than seven centuries and has followers from all castes and classes. This Warkari is a lower-caste person. Warkaris go for a particular pilgrimage every year, called a wari.

behind the car. He is between 30 and 40, dressed in a dhoti, a once-white but now soiled, tattered shirt, a string of rudraksha beads round his neck and a white cap. He carries a sling bag and holds a penant. Pratap stands in the far corner.]

SUTRADHAR: Let me describe this place first. As I said earlier, this is a square. A very large square in a very large city. It is very hot. This is a traffic jam. A riot has just happened here. People are in a foul mood. This Mercedes belongs to Yash. We have these two on the scooter, those four in the rickshaw and, of course, the passengers in the bus as we saw earlier—Achyut, Honap, etc. You'll get to know the others by and by. So here's a cauldron and here are the people sitting in it. There are others behind and ahead of this lot. Yash and Supriya Gadgil here are like Pushpatai. Their emotions are never aroused. I mean from the social point of view. But for their respective reasons. Pushpatai can't AFFORD to let her emotions be aroused. This couple can afford NOT to have their emotions aroused. Anyway, this couple has family money. They belong to the 0.0001 per cent of people in this country who have a TV installed in their cars which they can watch when they are caught in a traffic jam. Yash is very hard-working. He is a technocrat. He is Supriya's older sister's friend. Back in the day people thought something would come of the friendship—love and that sort of thing. Yes. But before that could happen, Supriya stole him. Prize catch. He is a reasonable man. But maybe we should talk to them... Yash Gadgil.

YASH: [*Rolls down window pane*] Yes?

SUTRADHAR: A couple of questions.

YASH: Sorry. I don't want to buy anything. And I don't give opinions for opinion polls. I don't have time for opinions.

SUTRADHAR: No, I only want an introduction.

YASH: Tch. All right. I'm Yash Gadgil of Gadgil Systems Pvt. Ltd. It is well-known. It is one of the biggest privately owned software companies.

SUTRADHAR: Isn't that where Pratap Chavan worked?

[Pratap picks up a stone. The sutradhar glances at him once but pretends not to have seen him and carries on. At some point in the following dialogue, the stone will fall out of Pratap's hand and he will acquire a dazed expression.]

YASH: Who's Pratap?

SUTRADHAR: I don't expect you to know. Anyway, how's business?

YASH: I sold Gadgil Systems last week to an American company. I'm starting another one now. I'll complete the formalities next week.

SUTRADHAR: [*Addressing Supriya*] And you, Madam? Do you help him in his work?

SUPRIYA: Me? [*Giggles*] No. I mean, I do in a way. Throw parties and that sort of thing. But that's also become so stereotypical. People like Yash don't need to have too many parties thrown. Just a few... But he shares everything with me, of course. His tensions and all.

SUTRADHAR: Any hobbies...theatre, music?

SUPRIYA: I used to love theatre. I acted in a play at college. I even belonged to a theatre group. Theatre Academy, it was called. I haven't really kept in touch. It's difficult to manage. Bhrugusi was too little...

SUTRADHAR: Who?

SUPRIYA: Bhrugudutt...Bhrugusi. Bhrugudutt Gadgil, our son.

SUTRADHAR: Will you go back to acting now?

SUPRIYA: [*Glancing at Yash*] I would love to. Bhrugusi is old enough.

> *[The sutradhar says, 'Thank you, please carry on'. They return to watching TV. A man and woman stand in front of the car and enact the interview that's happening on TV. The Warkari watches eagerly through the back of the car. The sutradhar steps forward. 'A car TV. Most of you can't have seen one. Please feel free.' So saying, he steps back.]*

TV WOMAN: How long ago did you leave Rajasthan? [*The Rajasthani carpenter is shy. He doesn't answer. To herself*] What kind of interview has Desai sent me out for. This bastard refuses to speak. Come on. Out with it. We have only fifty seconds. [*Aloud, sweetly but arrogantly*] Won't you speak?

MAN: Sister, it was like—many years. Can't remember. I'm just a carpenter. I am of the Salone caste. We're carpenters. But I find there is factory-made furniture even here. Everywhere. Nobody wants handcrafted stuff...

WOMAN: Listening to these people...

MAN: [*Cutting in*] Sister...on your channel you know... they have results of the Sikkim lottery. Have you any idea about today's...

WOMAN: [*Cutting in*] We have to go off the air now from...

[Yash takes the remote from Supriya's hand and switches off the TV. The man and the woman exit.]

SUPRIYA: Yash! [*Takes the remote from him and switches on the TV. The woman returns.*]

YASH: [*Takes the remote away again and switches it off. The woman exits.*] Shoo! Aren't we ever going to improve? Fuck them. It's just talk shows and lottery results everywhere. Not one goddam good channel available. No Zee, no MTV, no ESPN. Bloody native technology—

[Supriya tries to snatch the remote again. They struggle. Clearly this fight has roots that go deeper than control over the remote. Finally, Yash has the remote. Supriya's eyes fill. She gets busy trying to wipe them without spoiling her make-up and without Yash noticing. Yash isn't looking at her. He ramps up the AC, lowers the back of his seat and falls half asleep. The Warkari watches everything.]

SUTRADHAR: [*Standing beside the Warkari*] This Warkari's identity is a little peculiar. I mean he IS actually a Warkari. In the sense that he wears the bead necklace. But he is no longer a Warkari. Meaning that, along with being a Warkari, he was also a farmer with a small-holding. The Warkaris go on pilgrimage once a year in the month of Ashadh. So you might wonder what he is doing here now as three months have passed since Ashadh... Well, he lost his land in paying back the loan and there was no other work to be had. We know all the reasons for that—drought, sugarcane farming, the vast amounts of water it requires, the proliferation of cooperative sugar factories... We are clued in. Now this man remembered that when he passed through this city during the annual pilgrimage, people would give money. [*Pause*] So he has now become a permanent city Warkari.

[The TV in the car is switched off. There is silence inside. There's nothing to hold the Warkari's interest now. He moves forward, taps a knuckle on the car window to beg.]

WARKARI: Sahib, spare a couple of coins for a poor man.

YASH: Come forward. Come.

WARKARI: Sahib a few coins for a poor man. There's nothing in my stomach since the morning.

YASH: You look strong. Why do you beg?

WARKARI: Vitthal's will.

YASH: Did Vitthal tell you to beg?

WARKARI: [*Raising his voice*] Sahib, say what you like to me. You have no business saying things about my God Vitthal. [*His raised voice attracts the attention of others around him.*]

YASH: I know all about Vitthal. I've studied in a Marathi medium school. This type is what ruins things.

WARKARI: Sahib, keep your voice down.

SUPRIYA: Who is he?

YASH: A Warkari. But he's begging.

SUPRIYA: Why don't you give him a couple of rupees? [*Looks around*]

YASH: No. It's because of these traditions... Making Vitthal an excuse...

[The Warkari shouts loudly. A policeman arrives and leads him away.]

POLICEMAN: What's the matter eh?

WARKARI: This sahib here is cursing Vitthal. Tell him a few things.

POLICEMAN: Go on, get lost. [*Even as he is speaking, the Warkari is putting a mark of sacred paste on his forehead.*] Damn. He's done it. [*The policeman fishes out a couple of rupees from his pocket and hands them over to him. The Warkari chants 'Vitthal Vitthal'.*] Is Vitthal some relation of yours? Go. Get lost.

[The policeman nudges him towards the wings. The Warkari exits looking over his shoulder. Pause. Pratap follows the Warkari as though pulled.]

YASH: Havaldarsaab. Oh Saab. What's happening out there? What's the jam about?

POLICEMAN: How do I know Sahib? There's a line of cars as far as I can see. Maybe a riot like the earlier one...

SUPRIYA: Oh my God.

YASH: Shut up yaar. [*Turning to the havaldar*] Why don't you do something about it?

POLICEMAN: [*To himself*] What can one policeman do? It's these big cars that jam the traffic. These chaps make crores. Sit in AC cars. Create jams.

YASH: [*To himself*] If everyone in this country...everyone, works honestly, the country will change in two months. I work fourteen hours a day don't I?

POLICEMAN: [*To himself*] We stand in the sun for hours. These people make money for nothing. And it is we who give the Warkari money. And what salary do we get? Take a couple of coins extra and they're ready to shout corruption.

YASH: [*Holds out a ten-rupee note to the policeman. In a conciliatory tone*] Havaldarsaab, see what you can do.

POLICEMAN: What can I alone do about this jam boss? Why don't you find a way out? Weave left, right...

YASH: [*Angrily and in a tone of authority now*] Who's the traffic policemen here, you or me?

POLICEMAN: You're the one with a mobile. Call the control room.

YASH: Here. You call. [*To Supriya*] No phones for our police yet. [*Supriya is still upset. Doesn't pay attention to him.*] Shit!

POLICEMAN: [*On the phone*] Hallow! Control room?... This is me. Havaldar Ingle. There's a traffic... Who? Head Office?... [*Dials another number*] Hallow! Head Office? Yes. There's a traffic... I called the control room. They told me... Oh Rasta Peth? What's the number?... Talk properly can't you? Yes, give me the number... [*Dials the third number*] Hallow! Rasta Peth Police Station?... Listen there's a tra... Control Room? [*He switches off the phone and hands the instrument back to Yash.]* Bloody hell. Collection of asses! The whole department's full of them.

YASH: What?

POLICEMAN: Nothing. I'll go see. You keep sitting in your car.

[Pause]

SUPRIYA: [*To herself*] I have always been scared... Scared... Scared he'll leave me. What haven't I done to hold on to him? But he? Always wants his way. I won't put up with it now.

YASH: [*To himself*] There she goes frowning. Intolerable. She's totally intolerable.

SUPRIYA: [*To herself*] It's so frustrating. I won't rest now till I get one of those two things. I'll show him. My daddy has money too... I'll walk out. I'll talk to him. I've got to talk. [*Pause. To Yash*] Yash. I want to talk to you Yash... Listen to me.

YASH: [*Paying no attention and pointing to Seematini sitting in the rickshaw nearby.*] Have you seen that fatso in the rickshaw?

SUPRIYA: That other chap...what was he...the beggar. He was thin. He must have been starving. You fought with him. If you'd given him a couple of rupees he'd have eaten something.

YASH: Shut up! He was a Warkari. Not a beggar. You don't even know our traditions. That's the problem with India. You have plenty to eat. But you don't. Want to become thin...want to dry up like a twig. Won't eat. That's why Indians are such weaklings. Look at those people. Look at...Pete Sampras. They eat, work hard, digest. You only envy the Americans. You, that Warkari, your uncle.

SUPRIYA: Stop it.

[Yash shrugs. Pause]

SUPRIYA: Yash I want to talk to you.

[They freeze. The sutradhar cuts in.]

SUTRADHAR: I'll stop this couple on that dramatic note and proceed with the convenient sample I've chosen for my survey. A play like this will always have dramatic dialogue and convenient samples. And yet this is a pretty realistic play. What is not realistic is the representation of time. If you want a cross-section of characters time will have to be stretched. There's no other option. So let's leave these two sitting here. We'll turn for a moment to these two.

[The sutradhar approaches two men on a scooter. They are both around 45 or 50. Patil is more middle class, intellectual-looking, spectacles, bush shirt etc. Tamhane is more upper class.]

This is Patil. He's a communist. A cardholder. That's what people think. This is quite rare in Maharashtra these days, and who knows whether he really is a cardholder. I doubt if even he knows. Because he's a born communist. His grandfather was a communist. His parents fell in love in a communist study circle. The father was an intellectual communist. This one isn't intellectual. But he's a communist. You're born into a caste, right? Or into leadership. Similarly into communism these days, honourable exceptions apart of course. But he's a good man. Honest. Just weak in his thinking. Unfunny jokes. Happens sometimes. That's enough about him. Incidentally, this scooter is his. And this is Tamhane. He is both a socialist and a socialite by birth. His identity is complex like the Warkari's. He has inherited a business at birth. Mentally he's a businessman and a socialite. Emotionally he's a socialist. He doesn't exploit labour in his business. You don't need to... When you inherit an ancestral business in India, it soon starts running by itself, like a toddler.

[Pause]

The problem today is that they've had a little tiff. They're on their way to the National Archives where an Iranian women directors' film festival is on. They have been arguing about yesterday's film and the argument is getting a little personal.

PATIL: Look, religiosity simply won't do. Just because it's Iranian doesn't mean...

TAMHANE: Even Russia has supported any number of Islamic nations. I'm talking about Soviet Russia. All said and done, the importance of religion can't...

PATIL: Why do you talk about things you don't understand? You bloody call yourselves socialists and marry within your caste. If you find a Brahmin, so much the better.

TAMHANE: So should we go deliberately hunting for Dalits? That would be worse. Since when have you been worried about caste? When did you cosy up to Phule and Ambedkar?

PATIL: That was the last generation. All you know is to split. Split Marxists. Split Ambedkarites. To hell with you. There's no point talking to you. You would even split an individual into bits if he became a socialist. Huh!

[Pause]

TAMHANE: Even this joke is old now. Forty years old. You need to change with the world. [*Patil gets off the scooter and begins to walk.*] Hey, where are you going?

PATIL: To get a cigarette.

TAMHANE: What about me?

PATIL: I'll get one for you too. Has a socialist ever bought his own cigarette?

TAMHANE: So don't get one. Go.

PATIL: [*To himself*] Forty years he says. And what are these people doing? They used to split over ideology. Now it's over identity politics... Even their ideology was to show somehow that globalization had a human face... Curse publicly and sell the country to foreign banks privately... It's difficult even to see a film with this fellow. Must have a bloody cigarette.

TAMHANE: [*To himself*] Says we divide, the son of a bitch. So they unite, do they? They don't even join the government. Ideologies have become mere burkhas everywhere. Cuss words for America on the lips...American capital in the stomach. And we're off to see a film! With me sitting meekly on his scooter. Damn. I need a cigarette.

[The light now shifts to the rickshaw. The driver wears a skullcap. He is young, 25 or 30, enthusiastic and very talkative. He starts playing a Hindi film remix loudly on his sound system.]

SUTRADHAR: So that's the two of them. It's not just a traffic jam they're trapped in. They're trapped on every side, generally. Each is a blend of quick arousal of emotions and no arousal of emotions.

[Now the sutradhar comes near the rickshaw. In it we see the driver and three passengers. Ms Seemantini Nimbalkar is 35. Enthusiastic, tastefully dressed, very short hair. Ms Durga Khare, 65, cotton sari. Very simple. Stern expression. Mr Prasca Dora. Age 40. Jeans and T-shirt. Foreign labels. Dark glasses. Mobile. The sutradhar approaches the rickshaw.]

The same blend but for different reasons...one can see in Seemantini Nimbalkar. Those two are merely well-educated. But Seemantini is highly educated. A super-graduate in product design from IIT. Good family. Prosperous. Nicely respectful of things like socialism, Gandhi, Marx and traditions because she really doesn't have the time to give them a thought. She's a very busy person. She is so highly educated that there's no place for her in India. But she's sticking it out here. Her problem is that she isn't sure when it is right to let her emotions be aroused and when not. That's because she has no experience in social matters. She works with several NGOs. That's important. Because that's the reason why she's stuck in this square... This is how it happened. While she was working with an NGO she held a workshop for craftsmen in the Adivasi belt of Orissa to help them use product design know-how in their traditional crafts, to see if they could produce export-oriented stuff. That's a bit convoluted isn't it? Never mind. [*Pointing to the man with her.*] That chap...gentleman...is an Adivasi from Orissa. He studied in a mission school without converting. Back then, when Information Technology was in its infancy, he did his BSc in electronics. He won a mission scholarship to go to America. He's been there since then. [*Pointing to Durga*] And that's Durga Khare. She's a reputed scholar. She lives next door to Seemantini's office. Seemantini's mother and she are friends. She is single. She's involved in many social activities. She is a morally upright woman which makes her a little difficult for others to take. But certainly a woman of fine character. I mean in the modern sense. That's enough of an introduction. You'll gather the rest from their conversation. Oh yes and this, the driver, is Hanifbhai. He's obviously Muslim. You can see the moon and star right next to the rearview mirror, right? Seemantini has just spotted it and adjusted herself accordingly. She addresses him resolutely.

SEEMANTINI: *[Speaks in Hindi]* When will this jam break?

HANIF: How do I know Madam? I was caught in a similar one a few days ago. I was lucky the rickshaw came through safely.

SEEMANTINI: [*Continues to speak in Hindi]* There was a riot was there? Oh dear! Horrible. Why?

HANIF: Who knows? I ran into a small alley. Luckily there was a mosque there. I went in and sat down.

SEEMANTINI: You don't feel scared?

DURGA: Why are you talking in Hindi?

[Seemantini signals towards the moon and star and the number 786 and all that.]

DURGA: So?

[Nobody speaks.]

SEEMANTINI: Durga Aunty there's just been a riot.

[Pause]

DURGA: [*To herself*] This country has no future. This one is so highly educated...

SEEMANTINI: [*To herself*] She doesn't know what fear is. Why should she? Single. No children. Says what she likes wherever she likes. She'll get others into trouble one of these days.

HANIF: [*To himself*] I must read my Johar namaz. But how can I do it here? [*Looks at the passengers in the rearview mirror.*] Who's this blackie? Doesn't know Marathi. Wonder what caste he is. Sitting in style with two women. [*Looks at Seemantini in the mirror.*] Terrific arms she has. It's women like her who should wear sleeveless blouses. Not Ayesha for sure. What having three children has done to her! [*Looks out and shouts.*] Where d'you think you're going you son of a bitch? Eh? You think we're idiots standing around here you bastard?

DURGA: Kaka, remember we are sitting in the back here.

HANIF: Sorry.

DURGA: And will you kindly switch off that music?

[Everybody freezes. Hanif switches off the music.]

SUTRADHAR: I need to take a short break now to say a few things. Temperatures are rising here. There's a riot going on outside, so things are even hotter out there. Suspended between two riots. In limbo. So let me take this chance to say this.

I'd been thinking for several years of late that Mahatma Phule put down his ideas in the form of dialogues—'On Slavery' for example. Plato did the same with every idea he had. Other thinkers have done it too. We all know that. If we had someone who could write skilled dialogues like that about conditions today, it would make an excellent form of drama. There's nobody around with that kind of skill as far as I can see. So I stopped thinking about it. But that day in the bus, and afterwards in the traffic jam I realized that today, the nature of dialogue between two people has changed. There's hardly any dialogue. Only a huge chasm. So what use would a skilled dialogue writer be?

When skilled people in society become useless, the unskilled gain confidence. That is what happened with me. I began to see characters. I began to hear dialogues that were not dialogues and monologues as well. I apologized silently to Phule and Plato. I began making a mental note of the dialogues... Began creating my own. I could hear them all. Lots of people are stuck in this traffic jam now. As we saw a while ago, Pratap followed the Warkari out. Just then the traffic moved a bit. The bus also moved. Pratap noticed this and ran to take his seat. But that was all the movement the traffic made. It was a huge jam. Pratap kept to his seat fuming.

[Pratap enters and takes his place in the bus.]

PRATAP: [*To himself*] Damn. Stuck again. The Warkari must have gone away. Shall I get off? Let me wait for a couple of minutes. It might move. Anyway where will he go? He's a beggar. He'll stick to the square. It's my bloody future too now.

HONAP: [*Noticing Pushpatai's restlessness.*] Please don't worry. I'll see you home. I'll come all the way up.

PUSHPATAI: Uh no... Don't worry. [*To herself*] Wants to take his chance the lout... But maybe it's a good idea. The apartment block is miles away. A few bungalows in between. Good to have company at night... And all said and done, he's a Brahmin, after all. Timid. What will he do at most?

HONAP: [*To himself*] Today, I can go all the way up to her door. But Raunak and Sayli look at me like angry bulls. Damn... Should have picked up some chocolates.

[Pause. At the back Pratap slaps his forehead loudly. Nobody turns around except Achyut.]

SUTRADHAR: Before this, Achyut had kept quiet. But he had always known that keeping quiet wasn't right. One had to keep channels open. It wasn't right to isolate oneself or others. Even in defeat, one had to strive to keep the dialogue going. Pratap, too, had arrived at the same conclusion, though by the emotional route. He believed that one should be able to talk to others. Achyut was determined to ignore the difference in their routes. The resolve was further strengthened when he heard Pratap slap his forehead.

ACHYUT: [*In an explanatory tone*] See Pratap, the crux of the matter is to finally increase the rate of growth. When the rate of growth increases, wealth accumulates. So the government must create growth-oriented opportunities. Which means infrastructure, etc. The second need is to decrease government spending. I am fully aware that this is not enough. Accumulation of wealth doesn't necessarily mean it will trickle down. Nor can economic growth be equated with development. But the first step has to be the gradual reduction of the government's role in areas other than education and law and order. It is time to change labour laws in order to energize business and industry. [*Achyut's voice begins to fade away from here on. The sutradhar either sings or hums a lullaby. Pratap falls into a peaceful sleep. Achyut's words continue to be heard in little spurts.*] We have to become competitive... Our government provides jobs only for 2.5 per cent of the population... In America 8 per cent are in government jobs and in Sweden 14 per cent... Labour policy... Very simple... It is downsizing the government to actually increase its role, make it really more participatory...fiscal discipline... [*The sutradhar's lullaby has gradually faded away allowing Achyut's voice to be heard clearly.*] Add to that the fact that nations like America have over-subsidized the agricultural sector—

[The mention of America shakes Pratap awake.]

PRATAP: This...this is exactly what I've been saying. We must tell America once and for all...we are not going to tolerate this.

ACHYUT: How can we do that, dear man?

PRATAP: Why? Doesn't China do it?

ACHYUT: China is a different case. And even they bring America in by the back door.

PRATAP: We must tell the American president directly...

ACHYUT: What use would that be even if he personally sees our point. In international politics...

PRATAP: I don't like America. That's it.

[Pause]

SUTRADHAR: 'I like this, period'. 'I don't like that, period'. 'This is what I believe, period'... Then there can't be conversation, period! That's how this one ended. But Pratap was still simmering with his earlier rage. He wanted to beat up Achyut. He couldn't even find the words for a monologue. But just then he remembered some happy news. News that would stump Achyut in an argument and generally solve many of the country's problems.

PRATAP: Mister Athavale. I was watching breakfast TV today. They do news and debates, you know that. So there was this Delhi professor, some Guha or Phua...from the Gandhi something university...

ACHYUT: Jawaharlal Nehru University.

PRATAP: That's the one. And there was a man from INFOSYS and there was a model. The news was that the American Secretary of State has given Pakistan a right royal ticking off. Really put the screws on them. That was what the discussion was about...the things that will follow this step. I totally agreed with one point. That America is now likely to take our side on the Kashmir issue. Once that happens, it'll be America, Britain, France and us on one side and China and Pakistan on the other. It makes me like America. And in the end...

ACHYUT: That's not how it is. It's difficult to imagine, considering the Chinese market, America's South Asia policy and Pakistan's place in it. TV talk is just TV talk.

[Pratap gets up. He is furious. He circles Achyut saying the following to himself, gets off the bus and walks away.]

PRATAP: [*To himself*] Is this a man or the devil? He doesn't agree with what important people say on TV. He doesn't like TV. These days he doesn't like newspapers either. This pig doesn't even want America to side with us. He doesn't like anybody. He's ready to put obstacles in the way of everything. This chap has evil thoughts even about my job. Bloody ass fucker. Ass fucker.

[Pratap goes out.]

SUTRADHAR: So, as we just saw, Pratap left the bus to vent his rage in the traffic. How his rage will manifest itself, what will feed it, is anybody's guess. Will he meet the Warkari again? Let's wait and see. [*Pause*] But meanwhile, I must break off to mention one thing. Poverty. Losing jobs is terrible. I don't mean to ridicule Pratap. He's a good man. Ethically a little unstable. But on the other hand, it is worth remembering that, however furious he is with Achyut, he hasn't lost his senses totally... But none of these things count in identity politics... Sir [*addressing Achyut*] Sir, Pratap has gone out. [*Achyut sighs*] Sir, can a pressure group not be formed to help him?

ACHYUT: Huh... Sure pressure groups do get formed. But for different reasons—identity, caste...

[Short pause as the sutradhar waits for Achyut to continue. When he does not the sutradhar asks:]

SUTRADHAR: Don't you think this kind of identity politics which speaks in the name of empowerment will bring the country down?

ACHYUT: Just a moment. Empowerment isn't a wrong goal. Let me simplify. Reservation, for instance, isn't wrong. Allowing the have-nots to play a part in power, indeed to take over power, is an excellent thing. But democracy means something constructive that goes beyond these policies. Merely making advantages available...

SUTRADHAR: Precisely Sir. Here, it's only people like Lalu...

ACHYUT: [*Suddeny angry*] Please don't talk like that. Don't use a TV anchor's language. Sorry. I'm truly sorry. I didn't want to insult you. What I was...

[The sutradhar sighs and steps forward.]

SUTRADHAR: That is Athavale. He does his best to use his reason to keep his emotions under control. His is a very small category. He lost his temper with me just now. But generally his reason rules. There aren't too many people who share his identity. So he amounts to a zero in identity politics...

[*Glancing at Honap*] His value too should be zero. Because, although he belongs to the easily aroused emotions category, he is in a permanent job. He's a Brahmin. But when you have power, whether it is political or cultural, you do feel inviolable. He does. It is the confidence of belonging to a high caste for centuries. We've already heard what kind of housing society he lives in. [*Turning to Pushpatai*] Actually, she should carry the most weight in identity politics. She belongs to the emotionally not aroused category. In actual fact, her emotions get intensely aroused; but she's a woman and we know the place women hold in our society. [*Honap is staring hard at her.*] On top of it, she's single and responsible for her two children. Although her job is in a private company, it is permanent. She has been influenced by tradition. She sincerely loves those things that are popular and considered artistic today, like TV soaps and sentimental songs. Being a Brahmin and from the lower middle class, there are limits to how much she should allow her emotions to be aroused. There are many people in the country in this category, those who suffer limits on their emotional arousal. And endure [*Pointing to Honap*] this kind of terrorism. That is why she should hold a high place in identity politics. But that is not how it happens. Sheer numbers do not make a majority.

[Light fades on the bus and shines on the rickshaw.]

So we left Seemantini feeling embarrassed because Durga had been so blunt with the Muslim driver. Durga was thoroughly annoyed to see Seemantini feeling this way, even in this day and age. Add to that the crowd, heat and the cloying scent of the mogra malas being hawked and the fumes of the traffic jam. Seemantini is with Durga for something she needs from her. She was never meant to have intense conversations with her. She couldn't afford to have them. Upsetting her wouldn't help at all. So she said in a sweet voice...

SEEMANTINI: Durga Aunty, why did you go to Tambat[4] Lane that first time?

DURGA: It was to do with their problems with the local governing body...but why are you in such a hurry to go there? You said you'd tell me on the way.

SEEMANTINI: I was working in Orissa sometime ago with Adivasis, remember? With an NGO? So this gentleman is one of those Adivasis. He was away in America for many years. Now he wants to come back. And return to his roots. Isn't that great?

DURGA: What does that mean?

SEEMANTINI: He wants to start a factory for making traditional goods. You know those wire toys? I gave you one remember? That's what he'll make. I've done a lot of work on them. The same toys, but modified as aids for modern education. He wants to start a factory and export them. It will help his people a lot.

DURGA: So what's he doing in Pune?

SEEMANTINI: There's no infrastructure in Orissa, right? Power problems, labour problems...

DURGA:Labour problems? But won't he be using labour from there?

---

4. The traditional craftsmen who work on sheets of copper and brass metals to produce vessels and other copper items. Most of them are situated in a lane in any big city. Nowadays their trade is quite modernized and some have started factories of their own.

SEEMANTINI: He'll import a few hands, that's all. He won't need more labour than that. The factory will be fully mechanized. A German company has already been here to check out the requirements. They were thrilled. The factory will produce exact replicas of the traditional toys. They will retain the original energy of the craft.

DURGA: But why go to Tambat Lane?

SEEMANTINI: The Tambats have already started factories. He would like to see their craft as well. Perhaps, since he is starting a factory anyway, he could manufacture their goods as well... Just possible. Then he could bring more labour from Orissa. He can increase the scale. Our local people are very lazy. But someone from outside...

DURGA: That's utter idiocy. What are you saying? Is this the kind of work to do with traditional craftsmen? This man intends destroying his people's work, getting some ten or twelve of them down here and then taking work away from the Tambats too...

SEEMANTINI: But the people in his state are very badly off anyway.

DORA: What are you two saying? [*Upset because they are speaking in Marathi which he does not understand.*] Shouldn't I know? I'd like to be part of this.

DURGA: [*Shifting to part-English, part-Hindi*] You should be. You intend disturbing an entire lifestyle.

DORA: Oh, I have heard these arguments before...they have no value anymore! I don't agree with you at all... Are we to still remain where we were? Like museum exhibits? Why?... Tell me why. Look at yourself Madam, if you don't mind. I mean, look at your clothes. Why should my people remain like wild animals? So you can gawp at them?

DURGA: No that's not what I'm saying. You must change. I'll help you. Nobody should stagnate. We must all embrace modernity. But is starting a workshop here the way to do it? Coming from outside Maharashtra...

SEEMANTINI: [*She starts talking in Marathi again*] Durga Aunty, you are surely not saying that people from outside Maharashtra shouldn't come here? Like some people do? I hadn't expected a leftist like you to feel that way.

DURGA: It's not like that...

DORA: [*Angrily*] Can we talk in the national language please?

SEEMANTINI: It's okay Babu. Take it easy. We'll talk about it later. Alright?

[The Warkari enters. He approaches them and begs. Pratap is a little way behind him.]

WARKARI: Lady, I've just come back from the pilgrimage.

DURGA: Just? Pilgrimage?

[Seemantini gives him some money. Explains to Doraji, ignoring Durga.]

SEEMANTINI: This is a very old Marathi tradition. You should see them dance to devotional songs...

DORA: [*Cuts in, visibly upset*] Just a minute, Sister. This kind of thing happens everywhere. You sound as though you don't really belong here.

SEEMANTINI: No, no. I just thought I'd tell you.

DURGA: So don't tell him.

SEEMANTINI: But Aunty, you are forever standing up against all traditionalists. Earlier you were even telling him that traditions shouldn't stagnate and modernity...

DURGA: For God's sake, the two things...

DORA: [*Sighing*] Now what are you saying?

SEEMANTINI: Nothing Doraji. Nothing that's at all important. Sorry about...

WARKARI: Haven't eaten since the morning lady...

SEEMANTINI: [*To herself*] Talks from both sides, the hag. Actually she doesn't want either tradition or modernity. In fact, she wants nothing except to put down people. And anyway, what's wrong with giving a poor man a couple of coins? To hell with her. I just hope this one doesn't lose his temper with her. [*Offers money to the Warkari.*]

DURGA: Do you even know whether he's genuine?

SEEMANTINI: Tch, let it be, please.

DURGA: [*To herself*] These two coming together is the strangest thing I've seen. And yet both attack me...and how do they understand each other? That's what I'd like to know. These two extremes come together and I'm trapped between them... If her mother had told me what it was all about, I wouldn't have come. And this ass. Throws basic arguments at me... Why doesn't he move a bit? This isn't America.

DORA: [*To himself*] Sounds like a real bitch. Must be a Brahmin. Or some upper caste. They won't do a thing themselves but they'll talk about helping my people. It isn't enough for them that at least one man in the community grows. It doesn't satisfy them that one man has advanced. They want him to take the whole lot with him. And they say don't come to Maharashtra. That's great! Won't I be paying taxes here?

DURGA: [*To herself*] Move can't you? They think going to America and making money is everything. I bet he even thinks I'm trying to move away because I'm a Brahmin. What a jam this is... And I can't understand these two. Honestly. It's enough to make you wonder if you're living in the same country... How many jobs are these people going to take away? Money will come but go into only one man's pocket. It will never find its way into another...

SEEMANTINI: [*Senses tension and decides to cut it*] Durga Aunty I saw a documentary on BBC yesterday...

DURGA: [*To herself*] It has to be BBC for you. Your family doesn't get a single Indian language newspaper. Do you even know your elected rep...

SEEMANTINI: Listen to this Durga Aunty. Listen.

DURGA: Tell me. [*They freeze.*]

SUTRADHAR: [*Steps forward*] We've got to know all these people now. How many kinds of conversation have we heard? This play is just dialogues and monologues. It's not one of your conventional plays. It cannot be. These characters are not connected in any way. What holds them together is the overall theme. And the traffic jam in this square. The play is built with characters brought together by this chance event. [*Pause*] But take another look at Pratap. He is following the Warkari about. He is so confused he isn't even saying anything to himself.

[The Warkari and Pratap have reached the other end of the stage.]

WARKARI: [*Suddenly turning on Pratap*] What's up brother? Eh? What're you up to? You're following me. I've been watching.

PRATAP: [*To himself*] The rural folk are better off. They can become Warkaris. Not something I can do...dress up in a dhoti and walk around.

WARKARI: [*To himself*] Jobless...yes an urban jobless man. They own houses, have savings in the bank but no jobs... He can sit shoulder to shoulder with a Brahmin in a bus but he's jobless all the same... Let him come and see what's happening in villages.

PRATAP: See Uncle, I've lost my job. I'll have to beg now like you.

WARKARI: I'm not a beggar. I'm a Warkari. So what if I've lost my land? Vitthal will take care of my children. You don't get in my way.

[The Warkari moves. Pratap stands in his way.]

WARKARI: Let me go. This city is a dangerous place. I came out of a riot alive last time. I don't want to be caught again.

[Pratap moves away. The Warkari begins to leave. Pratap follows. The light comes up on Yash and Supriya.]

SURIYA:I need to talk to you Yash.

YASH: [*Sitting up*] Not about a child. Not about a child. Not about a child. Not about...

SURIYA: But...

YASH: We've had this out a hundred times. One child is enough. Don't want another. Switch on MTV. See if it's coming on.

SURIYA: I don't want to watch MTV.

YASH: You must oppose me, right?.

[Snatches the remote from her hand. Surfs. MTV comes on suddenly. The erotic song 'Aika Dajiba' plays. The audience also sees it in the form of a girl and boy dancing to it in front of the car. The volume is very loud, so the others on the stage also turn towards it. A youth carrying a bag, probably a college student out to have fun, peers in through the rear windshield. A policeman comes up behind him and drags him away.]

POLICEMAN: What're you looking at?

YOUTH: [*He talks in Hindi all the while. It is evident from his pronunciation that he is from outside Maharashtra.*] What's in the car?

POLICEMAN: Why?

YOUTH: Now if you have eyes you look, you will...

POLICEMAN: What's in the bag?

YOUTH: Not a bomb or anything.

POLICEMAN: What?

YOUTH: [*Smiles*] Not a bomb...

[The policeman hits him across the face. Then again. The youth loses his balance. Everybody freezes. Yash switches off the TV and turns round to look. The policeman hits the youth again and again, pushing him towards the wing saying, 'What was that? Say it again. Do you know what you're saying?' Yash doesn't switch on the TV again. Everybody is silent. Disturbed. Only Pushpatai's barely audible 'Oh dear' is heard. Honap moves closer to her. Light comes up again on Yash and Supriya. The tension between them is palpable. The following couple of dialogues/monologues reflect this tension as they stand still, with intermittent pauses.]

SURIYA: [*To herself*] Why should anybody hit anybody? [*Glancing at Yash*] He's so large...

[Her movements are like someone who is feeling claustrophobic. She's also trying to put a distance between herself and Yash. Yash is reclining in his adjustable seat.]

YASH: [*To himself*] That was some thrashing!... People simply don't behave unless they're thrashed... Look at this traffic jam. Some fucker up there must have barged in. And no policeman around... Someone does something like that, should be hanged. Yup. By the neck. That'll straighten them out... If everybody did his bit there would be no problem. Now screw yourself in this jam. How many man hours lost!... Go riot. How many man hours lost. The loss, the loss... What's this religion and caste business? Follow those things you fuckers. Don't we... Just hang them... We don't need theatrics—

SURIYA: [*Openly now*] Then let me act in plays.

YASH: What?

SURIYA: Let me act...

YASH: Let you what? Act? What for? Let's not go over that again.

SURIYA: No second child, then let me act.

YASH: [*Frustrated but in a pacifying tone*] Su, what is the connection between the two? Give me a child or let me act. That's ridiculous yaar.

SURIYA: All your talk of modernity is a sham. Vidya and I used to act when we were in college. She still does. She has two kids. And look at her husband. Looks like a thug. He's in politics. But he allows her... She's become a...why are you laughing?

YASH: I let you do everything else. Do I come in your way?

SURIYA: Then why not...

YASH: [*Suddenly angry*] Can't you let go of that one thing for me? And what kind of an actor were you anyway? Eh?

You think you're going to be a star? [*He has raised his voice very high. He's on the verge of violence.*]

SURIYA: Why are you so violent?

YASH: Because that's how I am. Now fuck off.

[Yash has become aggressive but hasn't left his place. Supriya has withdrawn into a corner. Then she flings open the car door in anger and bangs it shut. She walks away to the other corner and freezes. Yash sees her go and gets out of the car. He calls out, 'Supriya, where are you going?' Returns to his seat in the car and he too freezes.]

YASH: [*To himself*] So much rage over wanting to act? I can't understand it, yaar. What great things was she doing on stage? What's her problem? Go to hell... Where will she go at the most? To her father. Then she'll come back.

SURIYA: [*To herself*] Won't even let me act. He doesn't want a child. A child means irritation. As if he has to face it... What's his problem? Zilch. He just wants to assert his power... I will show him. Just you wait.

[Supriya exits. The sutradhar steps forward.]

SUTRADHAR: Irritation is spreading like a wildfire. But Achyut Athavale was already upset that day. Unable to stop myself, I asked him: [*To Achyut*] Sir, aren't you feeling well?

ACHYUT: Tch. I'm fine. Fine.

[Pause]

ACHYUT: [*To himself*] I don't know what's happened to me. It is impossible to talk. I spoke with Pratap. What happened? Where has he gone? I must talk even if I can manage to get through to the other person or not. [*To the sutradhar*] Yes, I was, I mean...

SUTRADHAR: Sir, you were saying something.

ACHYUT: I must tell you a story from the past. Say if you are bored if you are. I mean...but perhaps...no, forget it.

SUTRADHAR: No no. I want to hear it.

ACHYUT: When I was talking to Pratap I remembered my mother. This was in 1970 or 72...or was it later during the Emergency period imposed by Indira Gandhi in 1975... no, can't remember. But there was a hot discussion at home. Some activists had come to meet me. Maybe Yuvak Kranti Dal people and perhaps some others... If it was the Emergency then my sister wasn't there. She would have been in prison... Anyway that's not important. After they left my mother said to me, 'Why do people fight? Why can't two people love one another? I don't understand your communism or consumerism or whatever it is. But two people can live so easily together.' So I explained everything to her. In fact, I was a little irritated with her naivety. What she said was simplistic of course. But I keep remembering it again and again. I remembered it a while ago when I was talking to Pratap. Things are very complex. And you have to deal with the fact. That's what I was saying to Pratap. Then he went away, and I realized I just can't talk to him...I too get stuck... I must find a language to talk to him in. And to do that...but there's still so much poverty because there's brazen exploitation.

There are all kinds of divisions in our society, all kinds of inequality. One has to keep reminding oneself of that... You have to repeat this refrain every time you face this complexity. Otherwise it wraps you up in its fog... [*Pause*] One is aware of this. But one has to engage with people on this issue... People of the entire world. The same things exist everywhere...disparities, identities, media...the lot.

SUTRADHAR: But Sir, don't you think we should be a little assertive? A little more aggressive?

ACHYUT: Assertive doesn't mean violent, please. Yes, of course we should be assertive. But also tolerant. Some of us must learn to be assertive. Others to be tolerant. But it's never going to be easy... Things became a little foggy and I got confused. But I feel good after talking to you. I don't know...but thank you for listening.

SUTRADHAR: Not at all Sir.

ACHYUT: [*To himself*] Was that satisfying? Who knows what he was thinking. There has to be some communication... Both speaker and listener should understand things more or less in the same way... But still, there is some benefit in talking. A man needs privacy but he is also a social animal. His humanity is formed by society...I don't go with the existentialists. Or with maya and advaita for that matter—

[His voice is fading. Achyut exits. Honap has been trying to lay his head on Pushpa's shoulder under the pretext of falling asleep. Things have now gone beyond her tolerance. The light comes up on them.]

PUSHPATAI: [*To herself*] This has gone beyond all limits. He's pretending to be asleep... It's getting dark too. This fellow can't be trusted today. At night, the stretch that comes before the house is... If I start walking now, I might even make it. Move, you pig.

[She gets up. Honap is confused. She walks out. Honap follows her, calling 'Pushpatai...' They freeze outside the bus. The policeman comes from the other side dragging the youth with him. The earlier scene is repeated but silently and briefly. 'What's in your bag?' the policeman asks. 'Not a bomb,' the youth answers.]

SUTRADHAR: [*Comes forward*] This didn't happen a second time. It happened only once. But what we're doing is stretching time for us to see simultaneously things that are happening in different places. So some events will get repeated. Like a pesky thought that occurs to you during a sleepless night and will not go away, however hard you try.

[The policeman finishes his last lines, 'Bastard, you know what you're saying don't you? You go to college right? What? Irresponsible bastards!' He continues to hit the youth as they exit. They will say their lines a little differently each time. Lights come up on the rickshaw. Its four occupants sit frozen at the sight of this violence. Durga tries to get out but finds it difficult because the rickshaw is so cramped. Also because Seemantini is holding her hand.]

DURGA: He has to be stopped. He's beating him.

DORAJI: What are you doing?

SEEMANTINI: Durga Aunty!

[By this time the policeman has gone.]

HANIF: [*To himself*] Good he gave him a pasting. Bloody swine—'not a bomb' he says. The police are no less arrogant.

DORA: [*To himself*] Imagine wanting to stop the police. She needs to come to Orissa or Bihar once to learn her lesson. It's not right for a woman to be bold like this. She'll get killed. She's stopping us too.

DURGA: [*To herself*] Not one of them will move, fat lumps.

SEEMANTINI: [*Over-excited, in a shrill voice*] Durga Aunty, what I was saying was...

DURGA: [*Wearily*] What were you saying?

SEEMANTINI: I was telling you about the documentary, remember? It was about an African village. All tribals. You know, black...really really black people. And it's funny. They are also Muslim. See, when we say Muslim, we have an image before us, don't we? These people are something else altogether.

DURGA: [*To herself*] Everyone has an image...of Americans, of Arabs... And they vary a lot! Who knows what the images in this one's head are!

SEEMANTINI: A river flows past their village. For a few months in the year the tribals don't fish in it. Then one day they pray and start fishing. Mother said, this is exactly like arali pournima, which comes after the monsoon when we pray and start fishing. People all over the world are the same.

DURGA: [*Angry*] How can you say that? If you take the Adivasis...

SEEMANITINI: OK, but listen. So these tribals invite people from surrounding villages for the puja. They belong to the same clan, right? But the funny thing is, even when the other villagers are their kith and kin, they are not Muslim. I mean they are only black. Not black and Muslim. But black and tribals. Like the American slaves of the old days. And because they are not Muslim, they make such great tribal art on their pots and walls and doors. Pictures of flowers and animals and hunters. Fabulous. [*Durga's uneasiness is increasing. The policeman returns dragging the youth with him. He stands him in the middle of the stage. A scuffle follows over the youth's bag. The youth is scared but also defiant. Durga and Doraji's attention is riveted on the scene. Seemantini's voice becomes shriller with fear and excitement.*] So listen. A villager who goes with invitations to another village takes his son with him. So cute... These black children are so cute—they don't go to school—they are really, really cute.

[Now the Warkari and Pratap stand watching the policeman a little fearfully, a little mesmerized. Achyut also comes forward. Since the scene is taking place near the car, Yash will also step out occasionally. Noticing Achyut, Durga also comes out.]

POLICEMAN: Empty the bag. Let me see what you're carrying.

YOUTH: Come on Sir, let me off...otherwise...

POLICEMAN: Yes? Otherwise...[*Raises his hand again. Achyut stops him.*]

ACHYUT: Why are you hitting him?

POLICEMAN: Sahib, you heard what he said didn't you? Or didn't you?

ACHYUT: Certainly he was wrong to say that. But to hit him is...

[*The policeman stops him with a gesture. Meanwhile Durga has come near them.*]

DURGA: Sir...

ACHYUT: Oh hello...

DURGA: Are you also stuck here?

ACHYUT: In this bus.

DURGA: [*To the policeman*] You heard what he said didn't you?

POLICEMAN: Madam, please don't interfere. Let us perform our duty. So what's in the bag?

YOUTH: Nothing Sir.

POLICEMAN: Why are you speaking in Hindi? What's your name?

YOUTH: Ibrahim Choudhary.

POLICEMAN: Oh...a Mussalman... Choudhary is it? Eh? From outside huh? Where are you from? Bangladesh eh?

YOUTH: No. I'm from Orissa.

[Meanwhile, Prasca Dora, having heard the name, has got out of the rickshaw and is approaching them.]

POLICEMAN: [*To Yash*] That's how these people come here. Thieves. [*To Achyut*] Say what you like Sir, outsiders shouldn't be allowed in.

ACHYUT: But what's he done? How can everybody be bad?

POLICEMAN: Open the bag.

YOUTH: But Sir...

DORA: [*Intervening*] Let him go boss. Why are you... please come here a minute.

POLICEMAN: He was peeping into this gentleman's car sir. He's suspicious. Let him go he says.

DURGA: But that wasn't stealing! You can't immediately start...

POLICEMAN: Listen Madam, I know you...I've seen you in the agitation against the police. Remember last December?... What do you know about anything...about what we go through?... Now she's asking this brat to be let off. You don't see what our eyes see, okay? Our eyes are well trained. This brat's roaming about. And there's that Warkari and some other ragged suspicious-looking man... See them? Do you see them? [*To the youth*] Why are you gawping? Open up that bag. [*To Durga*] These days you can't tell who is siding with whom. You might even have a

Mussalman and Brahmin together like long-lost brothers... As for this fellow... He's an outsider. These chaps deserve to be thrashed—

[He yanks the bag out of the youth's hands and upturns it on the road. Amongst the assortment of things that fall out, there is a small knife and a poster done on the computer. The policeman picks up the knife and during the following dialogue, Yash picks up the poster.]

POLICEMAN: See this knife?

ACHYUT: What can a small knife like that do?

POLICEMAN: A lot. This is how it begins. Come on, you. Off to the police station.

[The policeman is about to grab him when Doraji intervenes. Durga wants to say something. The tension increases.]

DORAJI: [*Grabbing the youth by his shoulder*] C'mon, get up. Spoiling Orissa's reputation. Say sorry to him. Go on. [*The youth stands his ground defiantly. To the policeman*] I'll take care of this one. You carry on. [*To himself*] Must save him. Why do these young fellows get into these messes? [*Aloud*] You swine! [*Slaps him across the face. The youth shouts 'I'll show you' at the policeman. The policeman raises his hand. The youth stops his hand mid-air.*]

YOUTH: [*Somewhat scared but still defiant*] Hold it you son of a bitch. No touching, understand?... He's an outsider so bash him? Who do you think you are? I'll get you. Your boss will get a call today—my uncle is Chief Secretary in Orissa. I'll show you today what is what.

[Shrugs off the policeman's hold and starts walking away. The others stand frozen.]

YASH: [*To himself*] Bloody hell, what a painting! What imagination people have! There's no bloody art in me. Can't sing. Can't paint... This will look terrific in the bedroom.

[The youth has gone. As he passes by the Warkari, he drops a coin in his palm, which he has half held out. He merely glances at Pratap. Achyut has also gone back. The policeman is embarrassed and angry. He takes a couple of steps angrily towards the Warkari and Pratap and stops. He stares at Durga. Says to himself, 'Take a good look, yes. And go agitate,' and walks away. Durga mutters, 'Where is Athavale?' Then she and Doraji begin walking towards the rickshaw sunk in their own thoughts.]

DURGA: [*To herself*] What's going on? I don't get it. What did that boy say... It's terrible...this fellow bashing him up. What can I say to him...what am I doing by taking him to the Tambats and... [*Takes her seat in the rickshaw, very upset. Seemantini has been waiting, very scared. She resumes her story in her scared, hyper-excited, shrill voice.*]

SEEMANTINI: What I was saying Durga Aunty is...about the documentary...all the tribal art in the other village... the boy is shocked to see it. He's never seen anything like it before. Even though they are all related. And I was thinking, if we had been like that, all related to one another, things would have been so peaceful. And I'll tell you one thing. Craft...is even greater than our tribals. They are truly advanced, the tribles. Made me wonder could we not use some of these techniques and make products for export?

DURGA: [*Irritated*] But isn't that precisely what you are doing with this tribal gentleman? What exactly is your idea of being advanced? Who is advanced?... African tribals or our tribals or the Muslims who can't do these things or us?... This woman...impossible. [*Pause*] Seemantini, I'm sorry, but it's getting late. I must go. You carry on. I've called up Mr Wadke in Tambat Lane. He'll show you everything.

SEEMANTINI: But Durga Aunty, you've worked with him. He respects you—he's not going to talk to us openly if go without you.

[Everybody is moving, returning to their places. Yash continues to stare at the painting. Pushpatai's angry, weepy, controlled but cracking voice is heard. Pushpatai comes forward followed by Honap. She turns around and stops. Supriya is watching from her corner.]

PUSHPATAI: Please Honap, stop chasing me will you?

HONAP: I'm only trying to help. How will you get home safely by yourself?

PUSHPATAI: [*Faintly*] I'll manage. You go.

[Durga intervenes.]

DURGA: What's happened? Is he bothering you?

[Pushpa is helpless, speechless.]

HONAP: Listen Madam, why are you meddling? Nobody is bothering anybody. Go and sit down. I'm a government servant. A Brahmin. Go now.

DURGA: I was talking to her.

SEEMANTINI: Durga Aunty why do you want to...

PUSHPATAI: [*To herself*] I don't want a scene. Why make a noise? Dear me!

HONAP: [*To himself*] She had to meddle. What for? Why don't you go and sit where you belong, woman?

DURGA: [*To Seemantini*] You should be doing what I'm doing, girl. Look at my age and yours.

SEEMANTINI: But Durga Aunty, we don't even know how they are related to each other.

DURGA: They are human beings aren't they? You get it, don't you, that they are human beings? Or don't you?

SEEMANTINI: [*Bugged*] Durga Aunty you've had a monopoly all these years, haven't you, over saving the downtrodden? From poverty, from this, from that? So why is exploitation and poverty still with us? Why get at us?

DURGA: [*To herself*] In the old days these people didn't get it. Now they top ignorance with arrogance. So where's the hope? Okay. So poverty is still with us... But has nothing changed? Okay, so our methods may have been wrong. Then why don't you use your methods? What's the use of being conveniently neutral? Talking to this one is a waste of time, I must go.

[Meanwhile Pushpatai turns, muttering 'The bus is better than this. At least there are other people around,' and goes back followed by Honap. Durga watches her,

throws a furious look at Seemantini and goes out. Seemantini is fuming.]

SEEMANTINI: [*To herself*] No point talking to her. Always belittling people. Constantly making people look small. She has no children, no home to run. A permanent job as a professor. The same old cotton saris. No stake in anything. On her moral high horse. Against everything—against enjoyment, folk art, dams, Valentine's Day. Even when love brings two people together, she frowns. To hell with her.

[Pushpatai passes behind them weeping. Supriya is watching her, with her hand covering her mouth. The sutradhar approaches her.]

SUPRIYA: Who's that woman?

SUTRADHAR: [*After a long pause*] She is many things. She has multiple identities. For the moment, her identity as a woman without a husband and therefore available to others, should suffice.

[Supriya remains standing for a few moments. She shudders and runs to the car. Yash is in the car looking at the Odia youth's painting. Supriya enters and sits down.]

YASH: [*To himself*] What a painting... Here she is. Thank heavens. Didn't want to go looking for her. Saved the trouble. Enough to spin one's head. She was bound to come back but she might have driven me mad. [*Aloud*] See this painting?

SUPRIYA: It is fabulous. [*To herself*] Swine. They are all swine. In here and out there. [*Pause*] It's frustrating. Damn frustrating. I should see a film tomorrow or get a facial and pedicure. That'll calm me down. [*Looks at Yash. He's put the painting down and is almost asleep. Looks in the rearview mirror.*] Wonder if I should have a haircut. Oh shit! Shit! [*Stamps her feet and holds her head in her hands. Freeze. Achyut is very restless. All the actors now come closer together at the back. Their body language suggests frustration and rage. Some are cool as though waiting quietly for the quarry to show itself or because they can afford to be. The lighting will help to bring all these things out. Achyut begins to walk.*]

SUTRADHAR: [*To himself*] Every individual is separate, like the last grain of dust...atomized...and yet connected by an invisible but inevitable social thread...all separate, alone, yet unable to say of themselves that they are so, because they cannot bear to be in such a state, because their hearts break at the thought... I can hear my own voice in my head now...I need someone to converse with... Achyut? [*Aloud*] Sir.

ACHYUT: No. It has been the same with me. For many days now. I...sorry but...I don't know. A lecture is difficult to conceive today. I can't speak. But I'll walk there and see if I can gather myself.

[Achyut does not wait for a response. The sutradhar does not stop him. When he arrives on the other side of the stage, Durga sees him again. She sighs in relief.]

DURGA: Sir where are you going?

ACHYUT: There's a lecture. Or there was... I'm not sure...

DURGA: Can I go with you?

[She steps out without waiting for his answer and walks with him. Neither talks to the other, only to her/himself.]

ACHYUT: [*To himself*] I had begun to wonder if I find her more irritating than the others. But in the balance, I think she's more tolerable. Out of touch with the present. Still living in the 1960s and 70s. But at least living there... wherever that may be.

DURGA: [*To herself*] Athavale has changed. But he's still better to be with... Things are getting so claustrophobic... Athavale brings at least a small breath of air in. But that's about it. One can't tell from which direction the breath of air is coming. What is his ideology? Is he a Gandhian? A Marxist? A liberal? Postmodernist? What is he? In his last lecture he had posited all these positions at one and the same time. I don't understand him any longer. I will hear him today...but I'm sure he'll do the same again.

ACHYUT: [*To himself*] At least she is aware that people are losing jobs, that the economic gap is widening... She makes fun of me behind my back. She calls me loose bag... Raju was saying the same thing. Who doesn't make fun of others?... But when will these people come to grips with what's happening today in the world? When they face it they are thunderstruck. They are jolted... Tradition must be a flowing thing. This isn't true only of religion. It is true of Phule and Marx and Gandhi. Even then, Durga is better company than—

[Patil and Tamhane enter. Patil stops Achyut. They have bought their cigarettes and each holds one.]

PATIL: Sir.

ACHYUT: I'm off to the lecture. You?

TAMHANE: There's an Iranian film festival at the Archives...

ACHYUT: Oh yes. I'd forgotten. Completely.

TAMHANE: [*To himself*] Old man goes everywhere. And this Durga with him. At a play reading at my place, she put me on the mat in my own house. I don't read this sort of thing...you are the moneyed class...and this man kept mum. They are a pain. Why has Patil stopped him?

PATIL: Sir, Sohoni told me that you were making an argument against Chomsky's ideas about the media.

ACHYUT: Oh that... See, the media is a different thing now. But more than that, what he says about the dangers of people organizing themselves because of or through the media is possibly relevant to the labour movement in America. Here the divisions are very different... There's caste, there's religion—

[While this is going on Tamhane is bored and fuming. Suddenly he points towards the right and shouts.]

TAMHANE: Look. Look at that chap. Straight down the right side of the road. It's a free lane because the traffic is jammed at the other end. Jams happen because of people like him. Where's that policeman now, eh? Where is he?

ACHYUT: Should have been here.

TAMHANE: Such a passive remark is of no use... And that too coming from you! You're always nitpicking. Now tell us what's to be done?

DURGA: What's there to say? Everybody is stuck. So are we.

TAMHANE: Sure. But what's your position on it? You're always going on that we don't do this, we don't do that...

PATIL: Tamhane!

TAMHANE: These two really fucked me up that day. All I said was that things would be fine if everybody did their jobs honestly. So these two raised a question about compensation for work. The compensation I receive and what my workman in the factory receives. How much does he get and how much do you get? How can you say both should work with the same commitment? And this gentleman said working honestly doesn't apply only to your individual work... I had only made one statement... And here a law has been broken brazenly.

ACHYUT: [*In a raised voice that startles everybody*] So I'll tell you.

Durga: Sir...

[Meanwhile the sutradhar has arrived. He stops her with a gesture.]

ACHYUT: I'll tell you. Do you want a short cut? That's simple. Go to the next square. You'll find a policeman somewhere. Or go to the police station and sit-in. Protest. There's nothing that can't be achieved if a high middle-classer like you goes on satyagraha. [*Lowers his voice a little*] Otherwise the only way is what we were saying that day. That is to be aware. Be aware of the important issues of the day and to take constructive positions on them... It's no longer enough to split into groups, play identity politics, talk of empowerment. Because again the power will be vested in people like you. Or those who come to power will become like you. This is not a question of tolerance alone. Now we need both. We need to give up all this business of emotions being stirred and not being stirred.

DURGA: But Sir how can that be...

ACHYUT: [*Cutting her*] It is a long road. But it's the only way that even things like this—breaking laws, barging in—will stop.

[The Warkari has entered in the meanwhile and has come near them. He starts begging. Pratap watches from a distance.]

ACHYUT: Oh dear. Sorry... That was a lot of talking I did. I didn't listen to you carefully. [*The Warkari puts a mark on his forehead.*] Oh dear. I've forgotten my wallet... Pratap even had to buy my bus ticket. So...

DURGA: Sir, I don't give to beggars even if it's a Warkari.

PATIL: I don't either Sir. [*Takes his wallet from his pocket.*] But I'll give him something in your name, Sir. It's awkward when one is smoking and all. But not as bad as when one is eating ice cream...and one of these chaps...

[Everybody is embarrassed. The Warkari tries to put a mark on Patil's forehead. He stops him. He puts a mark on Tamhane's forehead. While doing this he unknowingly comes closer than he should to Durga. Tamhane, while saying 'But Athavale, how come you give to beggars?' pushes the Warkari a bit. The Warkari stumbles more than the lightness of the push warrants. Achyut extends a hand to him. Everybody is now near Yash's car. Seeing the Warkari stumble, Pratap barges in and holds Tamhane by the collar.]

PRATAP: Why did you push him, eh? Why did you push him?

TAMHANE: I only moved his hand away.

PRATAP: I saw with my own eyes. D'you know who he is? He's not a beggar. He's a Warkari. He is from the common castes... One of us. In fact, he's not even a Warkari. He's a farmer who's lost his land... He's like me. I've lost my job. And you pushed him. Why? Eh?

[A scuffle ensues. Achyut says 'Wait Pratap, wait', trying to control him. Patil also tries to stop the scuffle saying, 'You know this man Sir?' At some point in the melee, the Warkari dashes against Yash's car. As Yash steps out of the car, the Warkari gets knocked down again. In the middle of the confusion, someone else has suddenly appeared. This person has walked from one end to the other a few times in the course of the play.]

PERSON: [*To Pratap*] Why are you wasting your time asking him?... He's neither your class nor your caste. He's bound to have a grudge against our caste... These car owners are all the same... Why do you let them get away? Take off your chappal and hit them. [*To the Warkari*] You too. What are you waiting for? These are all city fellows. Get up and show them—

[Having said this, he moves away to the side.]

DURGA: How is he connected with this for heaven's sake? And how are you connected?

PATIL: [*Indicating Yash*] Don't you dare compare me with him. He's a bloody capitalist. I'm a communist. A communist.

[Pratap hits the roof of Yash's car.]

PRATAP: What difference does that make, huh? You are all the same. Who pushed me? You bastards. You make us lose our jobs, our lands. You turn us into beggars and when we lose our self-respect and beg, you push us eh? What's your name? Your name? You a Brahmin or a Mus...

ACHYUT: Pratap, Pratap. People don't have jobs for many reasons. In our circumstances it is true that one of the reasons has to do with religion and caste to some extent. But not in this way...not in the way you think.

[Pratap walks around at a quicker pace. Yash leaps out of his car and begins to talk of the damage done to it. The Warkari picks up his chappal and flings it at Yash. It hits the rickshaw, breaking its glass. Everybody

shouts together. There's bedlam. In the midst of all this, you hear some monologues and some dialogues. Voices merge. The following dialogue is heard against the noise.]

ACHYUT: Listen, listen. Don't carry on like this. Pratap, listen. The question is your job. I'll sit with you on satyagraha.

PRATAP: He isn't a beggar.

PUSHPATAI: But he's hurt.

TAMHANE: I didn't push. He fell by himself.

PRATAP: What's your name, you. What's your name?

ACHYUT: Look here. If you confine this question about people losing jobs to ideology or at least policy, then qualified people will come together and...

YASH: These people do these kind of things. They'll let the air out of tyres. Steal wipers. So they don't have jobs. Is it our fault?

HANIF: It's these cars that cause traffic jams. Is this a car or a tank?

PRATAP: Whose fault is it that he fell?

YASH: They're thieves.

DURGA: Listen. You can't make any old charges against them.

TAMHANE: What use is all this bookish talk? Real life is something else.

ACHYUT: This is just how real life is. Everybody who loses his job doesn't start begging. And if he does, of course those who made him lose it are responsible.

PUSHPATAI: Yes, but why fight? Those people have money. They are wealthy people.

HONAP: That's why the wealthy must be...

PUSHPATAI: But...

PRATAP: Madam, please don't interfere.

SEEMANTINI: Durga Aunty, why are we in this?

PRATAP: Shut up.

ACHYUT: Pratap, come with me.

PRATAP: He pushed him didn't he?

DURGA: Sir is right. A job...

YASH: These people don't want anybody to do well. Bloody hell. Let those who have money enjoy it as they wish. But—it's don't do this, don't do that...

TAMHANE: Quite. Everybody should be free yaar. This is a free country.

ACHYUT: Look here. This is a scary interpretation of freedom. It will boomerang on you one day.

PRATAP: He's made me lose my job. I know everything about him, his caste, religion. I'm going to cut off his...

ACHYUT: This is no way to protest Pratap. One day this will hit all of us.

YASH: Workers are work-shirkers.

SUPRIYA: But who's this man who's fallen down?

PUSHPA: He's a Warkari.

SUPRIYA: Warkari? What is that?

PRATAP: Let him have it.

PATIL: Athavale, your tolerance is nothing but escapism.

DURGA: Saying this to Sir is a...

WARKARI: Hell. I was better off in the village.

SUPRIYA: Only if roads were wider...

PRATAP: We should simply destroy this car.

TAMHANE: Do we call him a Warkari just because he's dressed like one?

SUPRIYA: But what is a Warkari?

PRATAP: You don't know who a Warkari is? In which fucking world do you live?

ACHYUT: Pratap...

YASH: No cursing.

TAMHANE: And why come here if he's a farmer? Why isn't he toiling away at his farm?

ACHYUT: Pratap—

PRATAP: You don't talk to me Sir. [*Looking at Yash*] This fucking...

YASH: [*Raising his voice*] If his emotions get inflamed so can mine. He touched my car. He reads sermons to others.

PRATAP: My job... Sir, I have respect for you...he shouldn't be talking to you like that.

[The noise and confusion increase. Nothing can be clearly heard now. The unknown man enters once again. He hands Pratap a stick and quickly joins the audience. As he goes Durga is heard saying, 'Who's this man who keeps butting in? Where did he spring from?' Pratap hits the car with the stick. Achyut pulls Pratap away and slaps him. Everyone freezes for a moment. Pratap is shocked. Durga overcomes her shock and walks to Achyut's side.]

DURGA: Sir you hit. You hit somebody. You hit Pratap of all people.

[Pause]

ACHYUT: Yes, I hit Pratap... Because he's the one who's going to suffer most in all this. [*Pause*] But I shouldn't have hit him...I was wrong... Now anything can happen.

[Everybody except Pratap, Durga, Achyut begins to move around. They come close to one another, want to move away but cannot. There is tremendous violence in those movements. The sutradhar comes forward.]

SUTRADHAR: All of them wanted to talk to each other, just as I did. And we have seen what happened. You can't understand the dialogues unless you can understand the monologues of the others—can't understand the spoken one sentence unless you understand the unspoken nine which precede it... That's the problem. But this is a play after all.

In the outside world, things have gone further than this. We, that is I and these actors, had no clue how and why such things happen. This was an attempt to see things for ourselves. Even now we haven't understood the whole of it. But we must end it here. I can resolve the traffic jam in the play by moving one person out. I will do so now. [*He moves one person away. The other actors move towards the wings at their own pace. Durga escorts Achyut out. The sutradhar remains on the stage alone with Pratap's fallen stick beside him.*] So this is how it ends in a play. But you will have to face the actual state of affairs in your own different ways when you go out. Namaskar.

Curtain

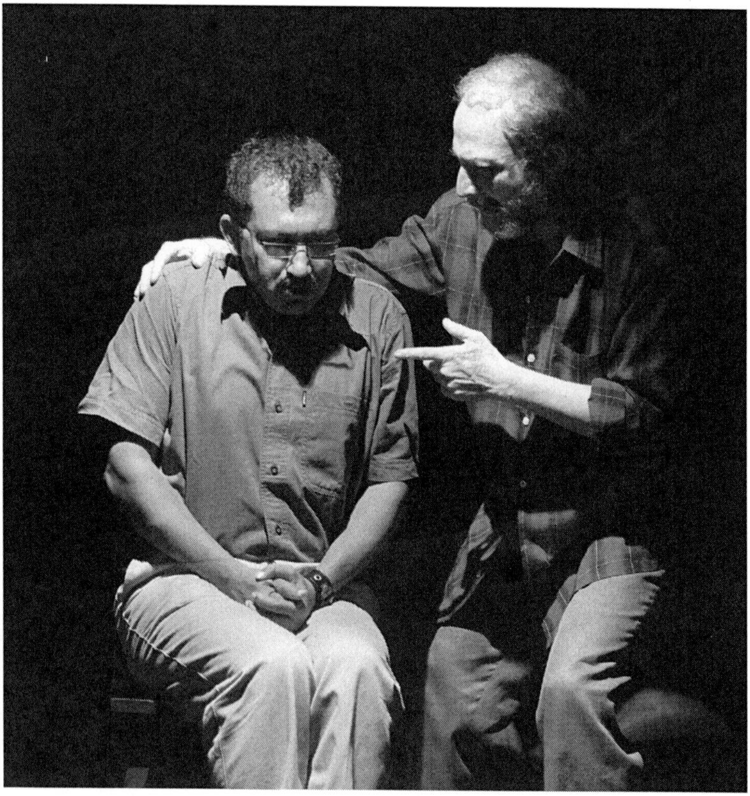

They Went Ahead
Still from the original Marathi production, 2007

They Went Ahead
Still from the original Marathi production, 2007

Crossroads
Still from the original Marathi production, 2004

Crossroads
Still from the original Marathi production, 2004

Crossroads
Still from the original Marathi production, 2004

The Man Who Saw the Sun
Stills from the original Marathi production, 1999

The Man Who Saw the Sun
Still from the original Marathi production, 1999

The Man Who Saw the Sun
Still from the original Marathi production, 1999

THE MAN WHO SAW THE SUN

Translated from the original Marathi play
Surya Pahilela Manus by Shanta Gokhale
and Makarand Sathe

Note: It is a well-known fact that Socrates did not write anything. Whatever is available has been written by his disciple and philosopher Plato. Some of the scenes in the play have been written with extensive references to the writings of Plato. Many translations of *Dialogues of Plato* are available in English. I have referred to a few of them while writing those scenes, as is necessary in any creative writing that is based on historical events and characters. However, the dialogues in those particular scenes in the play are not a copy of the original text, but a reconstruction. Nevertheless, I would like to express my gratitude to both—the original writer, philosopher Plato, and his numerous translators.

—Makarand Sathe

ACT 1

[Three men on the stage. Shadows unconnected with them hover over the back screen. Silence reigns—of the kind that comes at the end of a heated argument. ONE and TWO are restless. THREE is absolutely calm.]

ONE: Great. We'll get good and hungry now.

[No response from the others.]

ONE: Aren't you hungry?

[Pause]

ONE: I'm thinking of some nice hot...

TWO: Shut up, can't you? There's been a war of words here and this man is like nothing happened. Nothing stirs him. His blood doesn't boil.

THREE: We aren't admiring you.

TWO: Of course we are. Inner calm must always remain intact, come what may.

THREE: No it mustn't. Inner calm is not a chastity belt that it must remain intact.

[One laughs loudly. Pause]

ONE: Let's go eat.

TWO: While our blood boils, this one's like a slab of ice. [*Pause*] We will always fight. We will not agree about anything, anytime, anywhere.

ONE: [*Claps*] That's a fine bit of alliteration.

[Three and One laugh. Two is angry.]

TWO: You'll laugh at even putrid jokes if it suits you. But the best jokes won't move a muscle on your face if they're inconvenient. Then you will declare it as your political stand.

THREE: But it is. Everybody has a political stand. Including you. We declare ours openly. That's all. Even this fellow's taunting and jokes are his political stand.

ONE: At least we don't wave fine alliterative lines all over the place. Why can't you behave in a clear, simple way once in a while? Why complicate everything? Let's go. I'm hungry.

THREE: I've begun to find my irritation with you unbearable now.

[Pause]

ONE: So? We just sit around here do we?

THREE: Yes. Nothing is going to happen here. Make as much money as you can, like these people, and sit around with happiness plastered on your faces. Nobody will do anything. Nobody new will come. We will continue to see what we are seeing now.

[A man staggers in. Something dazzling appears to have blinded him. The three men rush to him and help him sit down.]

ONE: What's the matter with you? What happened?

[Four is dumbstruck. One runs indoors.]

TWO: [*To Three*] Water. Get some water.

THREE: Why don't you get it? You claim that your ideology is also about helping others.

TWO: Sure. But you believe your claim is greater. You'll try to turn him your way while I'm gone. Don't I know you?

[One returns with a glass of water.]

ONE: Here, drink. What happened? Did you meet someone like these fellows?

THREE: Like us? You will never even begin to understand our struggle.

TWO: True. But where did this one turn up from? Where are you from pal? Which world? Which time? What's wrong with you? This place... [*Looks around. Surprised.*] But where are we? This is not our usual place. It's different.

THREE: Not just different. It's weird... Once you notice it, you begin to feel quite terrified here.

ONE: I said it long ago. The place is different. Not just once. Half a dozen times, it's different, different...

TWO: Yes you did. But the very next minute you said, 'Let's play something'. You didn't even give yourself time to breathe. Who will take you seriously? You're a pain.

THREE: True. You want to be like little kids losing themselves playing with toy pots and pans.

ONE: Playing pots and pans is like living for them. Make your rules and play by them. At some point a flash of light might...

FOUR: [*Interrupting*] My eyes are gone. Yes. I think I've lost them.

THREE: No such thing has happened. Happens to us too sometimes. They'll come back. They are eyes after all. They'll come back after a while.

[Pause]

TWO: What shall we do now?

ONE: Shall we play? The old game? Shadows?

[Silence. Two and Three frown. Two paces the floor. Pause.]

TWO: It's this place. It's weird. People hardly ever come here.

[Five men enter from one side and go out from the other. They are Plato, Socrates, Crito, Alcibiades and Phaedo.]

ONE: [*Laughs like a child*] This place is really strange. Every time you say nobody comes here, some people come as though by magic. It's like reading a book and suddenly coming across a thought that has never occurred to you before. It's funny.

TWO: Yes, but who were they?

[Two, Three and Four have stood up, startled.]

THREE: I have begun to remember a bit.

ONE: So have I.

FOUR: I have begun to see a bit.

TWO: Did you recognize the man in front?

THREE: That one?

TWO: Yes him. That's Socrates.

THREE: Socrates! The Greek philosopher.

TWO: Yes. The one in front, short, bearded.

FOUR: So the one behind him, the tall man, must be his disciple Plato.

TWO: And the one with the aquiline nose must have been his friend Crito.

THREE: The wobbly-legged one has to be Alcibiades then.

FOUR: And the last one is Phaedo.

ONE: Phaedo?

PHAEDO: [*Turns around thinking he's been called*] Yes. That's me.

TWO: Now I get it. So this place is Plato's cave.

PHAEDO: Socrates' cave.

ONE: Which one's actually? How much of what Plato says is his and how much Socrates'?

[Phaedo laughs]

THREE: I can't remember everything that happened. How did we come to this part of the cave? I'm in a daze. I do remember the chains on our hands and feet. Nothing else.

PHAEDO: I remember everything. I was the first to hear it from Socrates.

TWO: Tell us again.

PHAEDO: We were all sitting around as usual. Socrates was late that day. [*Socrates enters*] And he started speaking in a most unusual manner.

SOCRATES: [*As he speaks matching visuals appear on the back screen.*] Look at this cave. The entire human race lives in it. The mouth of the cave is out there. That small hole. It is so small, barely any light gets in. People live here from their infancy, their hands and feet in chains, necks trapped in stocks. Nobody has any leeway to move. Their eyes can only look in one direction—straight... And can you see what's behind them? A blazing fire. That's the only light in the cave. And if you look carefully, you will see a wall between the fire and the people.

PHAEDO: I can see it.

SOCRATES: And on the wall cardboard figures are being moved. They are in varied shapes—humans, animals, objects. Their shadows fall on the wall. Some people are looking at them and gesticulating and talking. Some are silent. See them?

PHAEDO: The whole thing looks strange, Socrates. Even the prisoners look strange.

SOCRATES: See. They can look only straight ahead. They can only see their own shadows and the shadows of the cardboard figures.

PHAEDO: But what are they saying to each other?

SOCRATES: They can recognize the shadows now, right? So they give them names—mother, father, elephant, money, war... If somebody on this side says something, the wall throws back an echo. They think the shadows have spoken. Then they decide the future of the shadows. They converse with them. Now for them 'truth' is these shadows.

PHAEDO: That is so.

SOCRATES: Now see what has happened. One of them has freed himself from his shackles. He has turned his head. Now he can see the fire at the back. And it's light. Forget the shadows which he took to be his universe till now; he can barely see the figures that are casting them. And that man who has come to stand beside him, that's his teacher.

[Plato in the role of the teacher stands beside the man.]

PLATO: Get up. Open your eyes. Even if your eyes are blinded at first, they will definitely be able to see later. Now look at this truth. What you saw earlier were mere shadows. [*Shows him the cardboard figures*] Do you recognize these?

[The man is stunned.]

SOCRATES: Do you see that? He can't even remember the names he gave them earlier. Might he think, 'Yes, these are cardboard figures but perhaps the shadows were real?' Look now. He's being pushed and helped across a stony path through the mouth of the cave and out. Now he is in bright sunlight. Now the universe around him is the truth.

PHAEDO: But Socrates, he has been brought into the sunlight from the dark so suddenly. How can the poor man even see his surroundings?

SOCRATES: He'll get used to it gradually. First, he'll be able to make out objects that are in the shade. Then he will see reflections, including his own. Then the moon, the stars, heaven spread right across the sky and finally clear light and the sun. He will see the sun. Then he will see himself directly, not as a shadow. Then he will not think he is the cause of everything. He will see the light first. Then reason. And if after that he remembers the cave and his fellow prisoners there, he will feel pity for them. He will recall playing with them, watching shadows with them, competing with them, winning prizes and honours. But now he will not be awed by those honours. Rather than live as he did then, he will be willing to even suffer in order to...

THREE: [*Suddenly coming forward*] Excuse me, but I have a question. I have started recalling some things. Now suppose the sun you've seen, he has seen and I have seen are different?

SOCRATES: It is only people *looking for the sun* who come to this part of the cave. As you did. Such questions are bound to occur to them. Reason alone can bring the knowledge of all the suns together. You come to understand the real sun bit by bit, throughout your life.

TWO: But what do we hold on to meanwhile? How do we behave with others?

[Socrates does not reply, merely smiles and walks towards the other side. The others look at him. Suddenly he stands still in his tracks, looking into space. Plato and the others sit down. One, Two, Three and Four walk towards Socrates.]

PLATO: Don't worry. He's in the habit of suddenly becoming still.

ALCIBIADES: The man used to stand thinking like this even in the middle of a war. He spent a whole night like this once. When it grew light he walked away as though nothing unusual had happened.

[Socrates exits]

ONE: He did not complete what he was saying about the cave. What happened to the man who saw the sun? How will we know now?

PLATO: I'll tell you. He has returned to the cave, see? Coming from the light outside, he can't see a thing in there. Whether you move from the light to the dark or the other way around, you go blind for a while and in both cases people laugh at you. He is no longer amused by those shadows like the other prisoners. The prisoners will say this fellow went out and came back with his eyes gone. Nobody will dare go out now. Who wants to lose their sight! The one who saw the sun will become a laughing stock. Now others will say he's different from us. They will make fun of him. They will be irritated by the things he says.

THREE: What will he do under these circumstances? How will he live?

PLATO: This is how it is in this part of the cave. Some people don't know how to live after they've seen the sun, whichever sun it is. So what do these people do? They pull a shade over the sun itself through the way they behave. In the process they don't merely become a laughing stock, they cause the sun to be eclipsed.

THREE: So? How must they live?

PLATO: As Socrates did. Many others must have lived like him or died.

THREE: Died? What does that mean?

[Nobody replies. Long silence. Four looks lost. He is walking around, deep in thought. One, Two and Three exchange glances.]

ONE: I'll tell him a joke. Make him feel better. He's just come here. You do feel confused when you are new.

THREE: Is this the time for jokes?

CRITO: Any time is a time for jokes. It takes a while to understand that.

FOUR: I can't take this. Who are you people? Where have you come from? My circumstances are so terrible, even thinking of them makes me shudder. What is this place anyway? What is the use of gaining all this knowledge? It is useless where I come from. Nobody is bothered about moral precepts there. Life is meaningless.

[Pause]

CRITO: We have passed through similar circumstances. It is an extremely disturbing state.

TWO: Meaning? If circumstances do not please you, it's the end? Everybody is supposed to behave as they please?

CRITO: That's not what I meant. Even to understand whether circumstances are as you would like them to be, they have to be a little clear at least. At times even this much clarity is missing...We need to know what our circumstances are. If they are really bad, trusting another human being itself becomes difficult.

FOUR: Yes. That is exactly how it is in my country. It has become difficult to trust even your closest and dearest. You don't know who is honest. What is truth, what is falsehood. I could not even be sure whether I was mad or sane. So I began to look for answers. And that is how I found myself here. Now you tell me knowledgeable people come here. Is this knowledge?

PLATO: That's precisely the kind of people who come here, people who have been blinded by the sun. But don't be afraid. Our country too had become like that once.

Under the guise of democracy, power had fallen into hands that were rotten with corruption. Every society faces this situation occasionally. But even there you will still find people like Socrates.

FOUR: Meaning?

CRITO: Like our Socrates, who spend their lives tearing the veil off hypocrites, looking for the truth and living by it. Not allowing wife, children, friends to come in the way. Their minds are absolutely clear. They practically invite poverty upon themselves. That's how he lived, unconcerned about anything else.

[Four rises to go away. He is disturbed.]

CRITO: Wait. Don't be so upset.

FOUR: That's easy to say, but difficult for me to do in my situation. I simply do not understand how I am to live here, keeping my core and my sense of self intact. How do I deal with people? My wife stood beside me for years. But she cannot tolerate it any more. I feel stupid to say this, but people laugh at me because I think and try to live righteously. Earlier, they would laugh behind my back. Now they insult me to my face. My wife asks me, 'Why do you do these things?' She cannot endure the humiliation that we both suffer. So what now? Do I veer from my path and join them? And who are they? People who will normally not as much as look at each other, come together against me like conspirators. They are not bound by what we said the day before. [*He is beginning to sound scattered.*] My children are alienated from me. Thousands of people influence their minds. I...

CRITO: Calm down please. Sit... Sit here. Socrates' circumstances were exactly the same. I shall not go into the whole story. I will only tell you about how he was falsely charged and how he confronted the accusations. Listen. We feel reassured when we hear about people who have been through circumstances similar to ours. So listen.

ALCIBIADES: I'll tell you. I will start the story from the time when things had reached their limit. Or at least from the time we got to know about it. That day, Socrates didn't turn up at the square where we usually met. So we went to his home. By 'we' I mean the usual group. Only Phaedo was missing. He had gone off somewhere. There was a sepulchral silence in the house. Socrates stood lost in his own world. [*Socrates is seen standing still.*] We waited as usual for him to come out of his trance. Even his wife Xanthippe was nowhere to be seen. She always disliked our going there. If she talked properly at all, it was with Plato. We only wished Socrates would come to himself before she appeared.

XANTHIPPE: [*Entering*] Oh, it's you? Back again.

CRITO: Xanthippe, we are visitors to your home. Should you...

XANTHIPPE: Say thieves in my home. Spongers, lovers of grand speeches.

CRITO: [*Stops Alcibiades who is on the point of leaving.*] Socrates will not like what you are doing.

XANTHIPPE: Him? What will he do? Leave the house at the most? Take him away. Pick him up as he is and take him away. What use is he here? If I want to spend time with a few decent people outside I only get to hear ridicule and mockery. Or else people like you...

CRITO: Xanthippe!

PLATO: Something has happened... What...tell me—

XANTHIPPE: What happened? You have the cheek to ask? Forget about living like other decent folk, shouldn't I be sure that my children will have enough to eat? We don't ask for meat. We gave that up long ago. But shouldn't we know what we will have the next meal? You take him to feasts and listen to his lectures. And then you probably mock him behind his back.

PLATO: We? Would we mock him?

XANTHIPPE: You're the ones with money in your pockets. Rich men's sons. If you went to those Sophists for lessons, you'd blow up half your wealth. But Socrates is a fool. Loot him. Get knowledge for nothing.

ALCIBIADES: Socrates simply refuses to take money...

PLATO: [*Stopping him*] There's truth in what Xanthippe says. We must understand her point of view.

CRITO: Yes, go ahead and understand everybody's point of view. You are all for women. But please leave Xanthippe out of your sympathies. She sits on Socrates' back like some evil spirit torturing him. Shouldn't she think of his age if nothing else?

XANTHIPPE: Oh, his age is it? You're telling me? You're the ones who don't consider it. What will you lose if he dies? A few bits of knowledge that come for free. Pretty words are a luxury for rich men's sons... Do you even know what you're saying Crito? Forget his age. He's bound to die one day. But where's the guarantee that the people here will wait for that to happen? They'll kill him before that.

CRITO: What do you mean?

XANTHIPPE: Your eyes will never open. He's made so many enemies. We are the ones who will have to bear the consequences, not you. You can continue to live with eyes shut tight.

PLATO: Xanthippe, we were wrong. From this day on, all your household needs will be met. That's my responsibility.

XANTHIPPE: He will never accept that. Your uncle once sent us some corn. He had to take it back, defeated. Our youngest son was two years old then.

PLATO: We'll do it without his knowledge. Tomorrow morning I will...

XANTHIPPE: Great. And you call yourselves his disciples! I will never accept help that is sneaked in.

PLATO: Nor will I sneak help in. I will talk to Socrates.

XANTHIPPE: Don't talk to him. And don't tell him what I said. Please

[Flounces out.]

CRITO: Stupid woman!

PLATO: That's enough Crito. You are so full of resentment.

CRITO: What wrong did I say? It was for her benefit.

PLATO: Don't you see that Xanthippe is living much more according to Socrates's principles than we are.

CRITO: But...

PLATO: [*Glancing at Socrates*] We'll talk later.

[Socrates comes out of his trance.]

CRITO: Socrates, yesterday again in the Senate, a motion was moved regarding war.

SOCRATES: Rich nations are obliged to extend their borders.

CRITO: So are rich people, one way or another. Four cases of corruption were cleared in the Senate yesterday in a short time. Everybody was acquitted.

SOCRATES: You've decided to supply me with a news bulletin about the Senate have you?

CRITO: Mention of rich nations reminded me. Last time, speaking about justice, you had stopped at the idea of rich nations. I haven't been able to get it out of my head. Could you continue talking about it today please?

SOCRATES: We saw how a society and State are formed. We saw how the question of justice and injustice becomes more complex in a rich State than a poor one. You remember we spoke about what kind of men should govern such a State? Why it was necessary that a philosopher should head it? Is everybody agreed that we proved what we were saying up to this point?

PLATO: Sure. But you still haven't moved from the society and State to the individual.

[Alcibiades is staring hard at Socrates' feet.]

SOCRATES: The individual, like the three elements of society… [*Notices where Alcibiades is looking*] Why are you staring at my feet like that?

CRITO: There he goes interrupting. Sodden with drink as always.

ALCIBIADES: You are always ragging me. But look at his foot. He's hurt himself. It's a huge wound. Must have bled profusely.

CRITO: Nothing new there. Socrates will insist on walking barefoot and so hurt himself. It's been happening for seventy years. Who will change his ways? Will you tell him to wear shoes?

[Phaedo comes running in, looking frightened.]

PHAEDO: I've just heard the news Socrates. There's a conspiracy against you. A case will be filed tomorrow in court. Dreadful charges are going to be made against you.

ALCIBIADES: Like not wearing shoes?

PHAEDO: Idiot. Stop joking. You should have got wind of this news before. What's the use of being around in the Senate? Listen to the charges against Socrates. He lives a sinful, unrighteous life. He leads the youth astray. He is a heretic who rejects the gods of the State. He worships other gods.

ALCIBIADES: These charges are not only false, they are idiotic. This is a conspiracy, nothing less. They want to destroy him. If they had to charge him, it should have been for not wearing shoes.

CRITO: These are serious charges for which the punishment is death.

PLATO: Is the news true?

PHAEDO: It's from the innermost circle. We need to move quickly. We must meet people who are sympathetic to us. In Athens, there's nothing that can't be achieved with money and contacts.

PLATO: True. Once the wheels begin to spin, it'll be difficult to stop them.

CRITO: I'll collect some money. At least... [*Notices Socrates who is calm*] Say something Socrates.

SOCRATES: To do anything like this is to become one of them.

CRITO: But...

SOCRATES: I'm a citizen of Athens. I accept this. So I must obey its laws. I must face the charges in court. The charges are false, aren't they?

CRITO: False? It's a conspiracy. A conspiracy is false by definition. It is driven by motives other than justice. Why obey laws then?

SOCRATES: Crito, I am not so stupid as to not understand what a conspiracy is.

CRITO: [*A little abashed*] That's not what I meant.

PLATO: But we must do something, mustn't we?

SOCRATES: I'll give myself up to them tomorrow. I always knew this would happen one day. There have been attempts like this before. This time it looks as if they'll succeed in taking it all the way to a trial. [*Pause*] Anyway, we were speaking about society and the individual.

CRITO: Socrates...

SOCRATES: [*Ignoring him*] Do you remember the three elements of society?

PLATO: Yes. You spoke about them.

SOCRATES: Therefore, the individual too must be made up of the same three elements. If we cannot prove that, we will have to re-examine our ideas about society and justice.

[Two soldiers enter and take Socrates away. Crito and Phaedo follow them. Xanthippe is seen looking after them for a few moments. The lights dim gradually. When the lights come up again One, Three and Four have entered. Plato and Alcibiades stand in a corner.]

ONE: Death for such charges? What was wrong with these Greeks...

THREE: Nitwit.

ONE: Nitwit? No. Vengeful.

THREE: You are a nitwit. Not the Greeks. To lead youth astray and not to worship the gods that the majority of people worship are very serious charges. These things can overturn any government in any age. Governments will always condemn people like that to death.

ONE: This is dreadful

THREE: Politics isn't a game you idiot. [*Referring to Two*] Your are under the mistaken impression that you can keep the core of your life untouched while you play politics in the remaining space. You share this belief with this liberal friend of yours

FOUR: True. That's how it always is. That is what we can do. And all governments fear precisely this. They file cases against us, true or false.

PLATO: [*To One, Three and Four*] That is what happened. Socrates was arrested the following day and a case was filed against him. [*To Alcibiades*] And do you remember how Socrates responded to the charges in court? Socrates stood before the jury speaking in a plain, unadorned language—in Athens where rhetoric is considered the highest virtue.

[Socrates stands on the other side of the stage. He begins his defence. The audience is the jury. By the time the whole stage is lit, Socrates is standing alone on it.]

SOCRATES: Citizens of Athens, I don't know how you were affected by the words of my accusers, but they almost made me forget who I was—so persuasively did they speak. But with all this they have not uttered a word of truth. I was really amazed by one statement they made—when they warned you to be on guard and not allow yourselves to be deceived by the force of my eloquence. My eloquence!

Um...by eloquence if they mean the force of truth then I admit I am eloquent. I won't speak like an overenthusiastic young orator, in ornamental language. I don't know how to speak like that. But you will hear from me truth—the complete truth. I will defend myself in my accustomed manner. Like I do anywhere else...at my house, with my friends, at parties. I have only one request, do not judge me because I will speak in plain language, since I am convinced of the justness of my cause. Please allow me to do so. I am now more than seventy years of age and appearing for the first time in the court of law. I am quite a stranger to the language of this place. Treat me like a stranger speaking in his native tongue. I request you to discount the manner in which I am speaking, which may be or may not be good, but think only about the truth that my words speak of. Let the speaker speak truly and the judge decide justly, that's how it should be, in the court of law.

I would like to start my defence in a manner different from what I believe is normal. Because I believe that I have two types of accusers. One who have accused me here, in this court—Anytus, Meletus and Lycon; and the second type who accuse me outside this court. I am more afraid of the latter... They are far more dangerous...who began accusing me when you were children, telling of one Socrates, who speculated about the heavens and above, and searched into the earth beneath, and made the worse appear the better cause. These people are many, and you have heard their accusations when you were young, when your minds were more impressionable, and when there was no one to counter them. Hardest of all, I do not even know the names of these accusers. I must simply fight with their shadows in my defence. I will start with them.

They accuse me of teaching the youth, and many other things I have already mentioned. You must have seen comedies written by Aristophanes. He is one of them. He introduced a character in his plays that he calls Socrates, who he depicts as saying that he walks in air, and who talks about Science. These are matters I do not know anything about. Many of you have heard me talk. Have you ever heard me talk about these matters? You can judge for yourselves in this regard. I do not need to tell you about them.

They say I teach and take money for that. I really believe that it is very honourable if somebody was really able to instruct mankind and receive money for the instruction. Many people do that. If I had such kind of knowledge I would have been very proud, and conceited. But the truth is, I have no knowledge of that kind. Then what can I teach and how can I ask for money in return?

I daresay Athenians, that some of you will say, 'Okay Socrates, but what is the origin of these accusations, which are brought against you? There must have been something unusual that you have been doing? All these rumours and this talk about you would never have arisen if you had been like other men. Tell us then, what is the cause of them, for we do not want to judge hastily.' And I regard this as absolutely fair. I will tell you the cause. This reputation has come to me due to a certain sort of wisdom that I possess.

What kind of wisdom? The kind of limited wisdom that can be attained by humans. To that extent I am inclined to believe that I am wise, whereas the persons of whom I was speaking have a super human wisdom, which I fail to describe, because I do not have it myself. Here, men of Athens, I must beg you not to interrupt me, even if I seem to say something extravagant. For the words that I speak will not be mine, I will refer you to witness the God of Delphi. He will tell you about my wisdom. You must have known Chaerephon. Well, Chaerephon, as you know, was very bold and hasty in whatever he did. He went to Delphi and boldly asked the oracle to tell him whether [*at this point there is commotion in the jury*]—please, please don't interrupt me now—he asked the oracle to tell him whether anyone was wiser than I was, and the answer came there was no man wiser than Socrates. Chaerephon is dead, but his brother, who is in court, will confirm the truth in what I am saying.

Why do I mention this? Because I am trying to explain to you why I have such a bad reputation. When I heard the answer I said to myself, what can the God mean? For I knew I had no wisdom. I had never claimed to be wise. What then can he mean when he says that I am the wisest of men? He is God, he cannot lie. After long consideration I thought of a method of tackling this question. I realized that if I could only find a man wiser than myself, then I might go to the God, with a refutation in my hand. I could say to him, 'Here is a man wiser than I am, but you said I was the wisest.' Accordingly I went to one who had the reputation for wisdom, and observed him—his name I need not mention, but he was a politician, a man in power. When I asked him some questions, and I talked to him I could not help thinking, that this person, who was thought to be wise by many, and still wiser by himself, was not really wise at all. When I tried to tell him that he was not really wise, he started hating me. So I said to myself, 'Well, although neither of us is wise, I am better off than he is, for he is not wise but thinks that he is, whereas I, even though I too am not wise, I at least realize the fact.' Then I went to another one who had still higher pretensions to wisdom... And my conclusions were exactly the same. I just managed to create one more enemy.

Then I went to one man after another. I was aware of the enmity I provoked. But I had to consider the word of the God. I had to find the meaning of the oracle. And what was the result of my mission? I realized that the men most in repute were invariably foolish, and that the others less esteemed were really wiser and better. I made Herculean efforts to test the oracle. I went to poets. Tragic, romantic, comic, all sorts. They can hardly talk about and explain the meaning of their poetry. Then I went to artisans. Because they were good workmen, and because they knew about the things they manufactured, they thought that they had all the knowledge that one can have. The other thing that I managed through this inquiry, is that I ended up creating many enemies. But on the other hand and more importantly, I was able to find the meaning of this oracle. I came to know, that humans can never have true knowledge, and that only gods can be truly wise. Amongst men, he is the wisest, like Socrates, who knows that he is not really wise. In this way I go about this small universe of ours, obedient to God, from person to person—who is supposed to be wise, and show him that he is not wise. These efforts of mine take all the time I have, and I am left with no time to give either to any public matter or to any concern of my own. And that is why I am left in utter poverty.

There is another thing I must tell you at this point. Many young men who are rich and who have not much to do gather around me on their own accord. They like to hear the pretenders being examined by me. Then they often imitate me and proceed to examine others. Let me tell you that there is no dearth of those who need to be examined. Those who are examined by them, instead of getting angry with themselves, after knowing that they are not wise, get angry at me. They say, 'This confounded Socrates, this villainous misleader of youth.' If somebody asks them, 'Why, what evil does he practice or teach?' They have nothing to answer. Then they take refuge in the ready-made and arbitrary charges, which are customarily used in such conditions. They do not like to confess that their pretence to knowledge has been detected. They are numerous and ambitious. In a way those who have charged me in this court are, in fact, only their representatives—Meletus, Anytus and Lycon. Meletus represents poets, Anytus represents craftsmen and politicians, and Lycon represents rhetoricians. And this, O men of Athens, is the truth, and the whole truth. If you conduct an inquiry of your own, you will come to the same conclusion—these charges have come about due to prejudice and hatred.

I have said enough in my defence against the first category of my accusers, those who speak outside the court. Now I turn to the second—those who have actually challenged me in this court. Meletus is their leader. He calls himself a good man and true patriot. I request the court, his charges against me be read again—

MAN: [*Comes forward and reads*] Socrates is a sinful man of evil habits. Socrates leads youth astray from the path of righteous living. He does not believe in this city's gods, but creates his own gods instead.

SOCRATES: These in short are the charges against me... Meletus is an evil man. He will take a man to court out of sheer malice. He is not in the least interested in the matter for which he has done so. For him it is only mockery. That is what this man is like. I shall prove it now. I request that Meletus be brought in for cross examination.

[Meletus enters and sits on a chair.]

SOCRATES: Meletus, do you feel, deep down, any heartfelt concern for the future of our youth?

MELETUS: Yes. The matter is of great importance to me.

SOCRATES: You have accused me of corrupting the young and claim to have knowledge of their future. Therefore, can you state here who is responsible for improving their future? Everybody present here is interested in hearing your thoughts on the matter.

[Meletus is silent]

SOCRATES: Meletus, do you have nothing to say about it? I said earlier that you have not a shred of interest in any of these matters. Your silence proves it. You have not given any thought to it before accusing me. Speak. Tell everybody. You cannot be silent now. Who is responsible for securing the future of our youth?

MELETUS: The law.

SOCRATES: My question is about something else. Let me make myself clear. Who are the people who improve the minds of the young? In whose hands is the law invested? Who understands the law?

MELETUS: Judges and the jury.

SOCRATES: Are they the ones who give the young a good education?

MELETUS: Most certainly.

SOCRATES: All of them or some?

MELETUS: All.

SOCRATES: This is truly good news! This means there are many people who educate the youth. And what about the other people sitting here?

MELETUS: They too are good for the young.

SOCRATES: And the Senators?

MELETUS: They too guide the youth on the right path.

SOCRATES: Do you mean to say then that everybody in

Athens except me is qualified for the task? Only I corrupt them? Is that what you are saying?

MELETUS: That is my charge.

SOCRATES: If what you say is true, I must count myself very unfortunate. And our youth immensely fortunate that only one man corrupts them while every other person is bent on improving them. But Meletus, if you look around you, don't you think the opposite is true? It is. Whether it is a horse or man, it is the trainer who moulds him, guides him, improves his mind, gives him knowledge. Others either do nothing or create problems. Tell us Meletus. What do you think?

[Meletus is silent]

SOCRATES: This proves that you have made the charge without any thought. [*Pause*] Fine. I shall now ask you another question. Is it better to live with the righteous or the unrighteous?

MELETUS: The righteous of course.

SOCRATES: Living with the unrighteous is very painful. So would anybody suffer such pain consciously?

MELETUS: Why would he?

SOCRATES: Yes, why would he?... And when I corrupt the young, do I do it consciously? Deliberately?

MELETUS: In full consciousness.

SOCRATES: Now you had just admitted that one would be harmed by living with the bad and corrupt. You also state that I corrupt the youth intentionally, making them into bad citizens with whom I would have to live. Do you mean to say that you, with your superior wisdom, have recognized this fact, so early in life, that one would only be harmed by living among bad citizens, and me in this old age, have not been able to understand it? Meletus you will not be able to convince anybody with this. It means, that either I do not corrupt them, or I corrupt them unintentionally. And if my act is an unintentional one, I am not at fault according to the laws of Athens. Instead of bringing me to court, you ought to have talked to me privately and warned and advised me, on my unintentional wrongdoing. If you had done so, I would I have listened to you, learned from you. But you don't even speak to me outside this court. You bring me up in this court, which is a place not of instruction Meletus, but of punishment.

Your charges don't end here, and so I must continue. Meletus, you claim that I corrupt the youth. How do I do that? Is it by teaching them not to acknowledge the gods which the state acknowledges, but some other divinities in their stead? Are these the lessons with which I corrupt them, according to you ?

MELETUS: Yes.

SOCRATES: Meletus, take an oath on the gods we are speaking of and explain your charges to me. Truly I cannot understand them. Do I not believe in the gods of this city? Or do I believe in some other gods altogether? Or do I not believe in any god at all and I am an atheist? What exactly is your charge?

MELETUS: That you are an atheist. You do not believe in any god.

SOCRATES: What a strange statement. Does that mean I do not believe even in the sun and the moon?

MELETUS: Members of the jury, I wish to make a strong statement here that Socrates has been saying the sun is made of stone and the moon of mud.

SOCRATES: Oh but you are talking about Aristophenes, not me. Have you forgotten who the accused is? I do not say any such thing. The Socrates in Aristophenes' play does. People pay good money to hear him say such things which make them laugh. Do you think this jury will not know even this much? Aristophenes' books are filled with things like this. Have you ever heard me say this? And yet you maintain your charge that I am an atheist?

MELETUS: Yes, you are an atheist out and out.

SOCRATES: It does appear that there is a contradiction in what you are saying. You are saying that I believe in gods and I am an atheist at the same time...[*Commotion in the jury again.*] Please, please, I remind you of my request of not interrupting me if I speak in my own manner. Please allow me to continue, as I now intend to prove that there is contradiction in what he says. Meletus, can one ever believe in the existence of the things made by men and not in human beings who made them to start with? I wish, men of Athens, that he answers, and will not always be trying to interrupt. Similarly, can ever any man believe in horsemanship, and not in horses? Or in flute playing and not in flute-player?...

[Meletus does not answer]

SOCRATES: I will answer on your behalf. This is impossible. Now answer my next question. You have said in your charge sheet that I believe in spiritual and divine agencies, right? Now what is the source of these forces? Who do they belong to? They belong to the spirits and demigods don't they? If I believe in these forces, I must surely believe in those spirits and demigods too. No?

MELETUS: Yes, the fact that you believe in those forces means you believe in celestial spirits and demigods too.

SOCRATES: Thank you for your answer. Now tell me, are these spirits and demigods not the children, whichever way they were born, of this city's deities?

MELETUS: Yes.

SOCRATES: That means I believe in them too? If you believe in the existence of children, you perforce believe in the existence of their parents. Would anybody say, 'I believe mules exist but I don't believe horses and donkeys exist?' You puzzle me by claiming two opposing things—'He does not believe in god' and 'He believes in god.' The reason for this is that you have no real accusation to make against me.

[Meletus exits. Socrates turns to the audience. Socrates is alone on the stage.]

SOCRATES: I have said enough in answer to the charges of Meletus. But I know only too well how many enemies I have created. And their envy may well be the cause of my destruction. This envy has brought death to many a good man in the past, and will probably do the same to many more in the future. There is no danger of me being the last of them. Anyway, one should not be afraid of death. A man who is good for anything ought not to calculate the chances of living or dying while making moral decisions. I faced death every time you sent me to war. God orders me to fulfil the philosopher's mission of searching into myself and other men. It would indeed be wrong, if I were to desert my post now due to the fear of death. If I do so, it would indeed then be justifiable to bring me to court on the charges of disobeying god. For the fear of death is indeed nothing but a pretence of wisdom.

On the other hand, if you are going to let me go, please do so without any conditions. You may say, 'Socrates, this time we will not mind Meletus and Anytus, and you shall be let off, but on one condition, that you are not to inquire and speculate in this way anymore, and that if you are caught doing so again, you shall die.' But though I love and honour you, O citizens of Athens, I shall obey god rather than you. And while I have life and strength, I will never cease from the practice and teaching of philosophy. I will go on asking every man I meet, 'You my friend, a citizen of the great Athens, are you not ashamed of collecting the greatest amount of money and honour and reputation, and caring so little about wisdom and truth and the improvement of the soul?' I will go on asking this and examining each and every person I meet, especially here in Athens, because this is my city, and Athenians are my brethren. Whether you acquit me or not, understand that I will never alter my ways, not even if I have to die many times.

Men of Athens, do not interrupt me. There was an understanding between us that you should hear me to the end and I have something more to say. If you kill such a man as I, you will injure yourself more than you will injure me. I am a gadfly given to the State by god. If you kill me you will not easily find a successor to me. State is like a great and noble steed that is lazy in his motions. It requires to be stirred to life. I am that gadfly who god has attached to the State, arousing, persuading, and reproaching you. If I had been like other men, I should not have neglected all my concerns about my own welfare, and I would not have come to you individually like a father or elder brother, exhorting you to regard virtue. If I had gained anything by doing this, it could have been interpreted in a different manner. But not even the impudence of my accusers dare charge me for any payments and gains from my activities. I have sufficient proof to the truth of what I say—my perpetual poverty.

Some of you may wonder why I go about in private giving advice, and busying myself with the concerns of the others, but not assume any public office. You must have heard me speak of an oracle or sign which comes to me, the divinity which Meletus ridicules in his indictment. The sign, which is a kind of an inner voice, forbids me from becoming a politician and striving for any public post of power. I am certain that if I were in politics I would have perished long ago. It has to be done privately. For following my vow to follow the road of truth, I was on the verge of being eliminated twice in the past. Once...but you are well aware of that history. Can anybody ever assume an office and refuse to yield or leave the path of truth simultaneously? Never, it is not possible.

Here I would like to call on those whom I am supposed to have corrupted in youth, and are now old enough to judge for themselves, to come forward and give evidence if they think their families have suffered at my hands. If they do not want to do this themselves for some reason or other, I call upon their fathers, brothers, relatives and friends to do so. Many of them I see in the court. There is Crito, there is Critobulus, his son. I can also see Lysanius, Antiphon, Epigenes, Plato and so many others. Some of whom Meletus should have presented as witnesses. I give him one more chance if he wants to do so. Meletus—[*Calling Meletus, Socrates waits for him to come, but nobody comes forward.*] It seems that Meletus knows that these witnesses would go against him. What more proof is required to decide if the truth is on Meletus' side or mine?

One more word before I conclude my defence. I will not present my wife, relatives and sons here, who through their grief and crying are supposed to make a plea for my acquittal. I, too, have a family. I have three young sons. I have seen many respected people follow this tradition. Whether I am or am not afraid of death is another question. I feel such conduct would be discreditable to myself and to you. It is quite in order to state your case properly. But to ask the judges for favours is totally condemnable, for their duty is not to make a present of justice, but to give judgment. There can be no piety in that. Do not then require me to do what I consider dishonourable and wrong. In fact, I request you to discontinue this tradition, once for all. I believe in god. I leave decision about my future to you and to the god. I believe you will do what is good for me and for you, and what is just.

[Socrates goes to a corner and freezes. Lights slowly dim. Curtain.]

End of Act I

ACT II

[ONE, TWO, THREE, FOUR are on a fully lit stage.]

ONE: Then what happened? Where are they? They've left us hanging in the middle of the story about the man who saw the sun. What happened to Socrates after this?

FOUR: And to the others too. Did they follow him to see the sun? Or did they return to the shadows? Or did they remain suspended in the middle?

ONE: You are seeing things better it seems.

FOUR: Huh.

[Pause]

ONE: Where are they?

[Xanthippe enters from the left and exits to the right.]

THREE: What's Xanthippe doing here?

FOUR: Does she not have the right to come here?

TWO: But only... [*Brief pause*]

FOUR: Go on... 'But only some people come here.' As though only some may receive knowledge. Wise people never separate knowledge from practice... Which means that everybody is capable of acquiring knowledge. That is why Socrates used to walk around the city's squares and public places talking to the people. That is why he said a while ago that it is the people who have real knowledge.

THREE: But why is Xanthippe here? Only because she is Socrates' wife? The truth is that men who want to achieve something in public life shouldn't marry. I said this once before remember? [*To Two*] You fought with me then.

TWO: How did Xanthippe trouble Socrates?

THREE: Did she not? Throughout his life? And now she traipses around here just because she is his wife! [*Indicating Four*] And he? Just a while ago he was talking helplessly about having a wife and children.

FOUR: [*Suddenly stands up*] That has nothing to do with this. This is a completely different question.

THREE: How is it different? H'm?

[Four stands apart without saying a word. The others look at him. Alcibiades enters.]

TWO: We'll talk later.

FOUR: No, you carry on. Don't let me stop you.

ALCIBIADES: Stop you from what?

THREE: I was only saying...

ONE: We'll talk later. [*Pause. To Alcibiades*] Back in the Senate when Socrates was arguing his case, all of you walked out towards the end. Why was that?

ALCIBIADES: Because people were gathering outside. They needed to be reassured. Meletus had appointed armed guards out there.

ONE: So then?

ALCIBIADES: We were also making other preparations. People didn't know which way things would go.

THREE: The time was right for an uprising.

ALCIBIADES: It would have been difficult to bring it about in Athens. The whole system was different there. Many of the people were in the Senate. Who knew how many of them were turncoats.

THREE: Be damned then. You can't afford to miss opportunities in politics.

ALCIBIADES: We weren't missing opportunities. But we needed to figure out what Socrates would want or not want, didn't we? That was our biggest problem.

FOUR: [*Whirling around*] But what were *you* thinking. Clichéd sayings like 'don't miss opportunities' and 'think before you act', don't serve much purpose. What were your thoughts? What is the best thing to do at such times, or at any time for that matter?

ALCIBIADES: It was a strange situation. Quite unusual. It was difficult to decide.

FOUR: So then?

THREE: So then? Even I can tell you that. People split into two groups.

ALCIBIADES: Yes.

THREE: Then silence reigned.

ALCIBIADES: Yes.

[Pause]

FOUR: But what actually happened?

THREE: What could happen?

[Alcibiades looks helpless. He has no answer. Now Plato, Crito, etc enter.]

ALCIBIADES: [*To Plato, indicating Four*] Good you've come. This one's been asking too many questions. Like Socrates.

TWO: What happened in the Senate? What was the judgment?

ONE: Wait. [*To Plato*] There's that story you left incomplete. A man returned to the dark from the light. He could not see anything. People mocked him. What happened next?

[Again we see the cave. Scenes illustrating what Plato says appear at the back.]

PLATO: Next? He was able to see a little at a time. He began talking. Explaining to people. Some people began to be annoyed by him. It is clear now that he is going to unshackle and liberate somebody else. It won't be long before people arrest him and then it will be death for him. How can they afford to have him in their midst? Some people don't want truth because it goes against their interests. Others don't want it because they are ignorant. You wanted to know what the judgment was, didn't you? Socrates was sentenced to death.

TWO: But wasn't there a law in Athens that allowed a

man to escape a death sentence by paying a fine? Was Socrates not offered that loophole?

PLATO: Why not? The offer was certainly made.

[Socrates stands to one side with the light on him. The others leave.]

SOCRATES: Death sentence! There are many reasons why I am not grieved at the vote of condemnation. I expected it. I am only surprised that the decision went against me by only thirty votes. Conditions are better than I imagined. If Lycon and Anytus had not supported Meletus, the decision would surely have gone in my favour, and according to the law, it would have been Meletus who would have had to a pay a fine.

Meletus proposes death as the penalty. What shall I propose on my part? What is my due? What should be the value of a man's life who never sat idle during his whole life, but was careless about wealth and honours and family interests? What would be the value of man's life, who is your benefactor and who tried to instruct according to his capacities? Why am I talking about this, after what I said about tears and prayers? I speak because I am convinced that I have never intentionally wronged anyone; it is different matter that I cannot convince you of that—the time has been too short. If there were a law in Athens, as there is in other cities, that a capital case should not be decided in one day, then I believe I would have been able to convince you.

I am convinced myself that I have never wronged another... I should not wrong myself either. Why should I? Because I am afraid of the penalty of death?... I am sure that a fine, or imprisonment, is evil and bad. And I do not know if death is good or evil. Anyway if it is imprisonment till I am able to pay the fine then it means imprisonment for life, as I have no money to pay the fine. And as I said that is evil. And if I say exile, I must indeed be blinded by the love of life. Because it will mean that I am so irrational as to expect that others will tolerate and like my behaviour and discourses, when you, who are from my own city, cannot do so. No, that is not very likely. And what a life would I lead then, wandering from city to city, always being driven out. For I am quite sure that wherever I go, young men would gather around me, that I will not stop my pursuit of truth, and in the end I will be driven out. I will go on behaving like this because it is the wish of god. My life would be meaningless if I stop examining myself and others. But I must respect your wishes. I propose that thirty minae be the penalty. Plato, Crito, and Critobulus will stand as sureties. I assume that for thirty minae these many sureties are certainly enough.

[Gradually the light on Socrates fades. Light comes up on the people in the cave.]

THREE: He offered to pay only thirty minae? Was Socrates offering to pay a fine or was he playing a joke on them?

PLATO: How much do you think he should have offered?

THREE: Any amount. You were there. Did you not feel responsible? It is vital to keep men like Socrates alive. If he lives, much can change. There are times when such political decisions must be taken. Socrates must live.

PLATO: Does Socrates ever live by paying a fine? A man named Socrates might. But that would not be the real Socrates. Socrates lives not by his ideas alone but by his practice of those ideas. All ideologies, all theories are proved by the acts they inspire. This was his firm belief.

FOUR: Did they accept a fine of thirty minae?

PLATO: How could they? That would have been laughable.

FOUR: So then?

PLATO: Then? They allowed Socrates to speak again. At least that.

[Light on Socrates again. The others are in the dark.]

SOCRATES: Citizens of Athens, if you had shown a little patience, your desire to see me dead would have been fulfilled by the course of nature, so advanced am I in years. Do you know what will happen now? Your detractors in the city will always reproach you saying, 'You killed Socrates, a wise man.' Not only good men will do so, but even the bad ones will conveniently use this opportunity. Only if you had waited for some time—and I am not speaking now to all of you, but only to those who have condemned me to death—this wish would have been naturally fulfilled!...

I do not repent my style of defence. One should not be afraid of death, either in war or in the matters of justice. The question my friends, is not how to avoid death, but how to avoid unrighteousness...

In the hour of death, men are said to be gifted with powers to prophesize. I too can make a prophesy, as I can clearly see what is going to happen in future... A punishment far heavier than you have inflicted on me, awaits you in future. As your accusers will be younger they will be far more inconsiderate. You have condemned me to death because you wanted to escape the wrath of my accusers, and not because you followed your conscience. Your accusers will be harsher. If you think you can prevent someone from censuring your evil lives by killing him, you are mistaken.

Friends who have voted for my acquittal, I would also like to talk to you. The oracle which I have already talked about did not stop me even once today. There can be only one meaning of this, whatever has happened to me today is not a bad thing, and I behaved correctly. It means that death is a good thing. What is death? Death is one of the two things—either it is nothingness or it is the migration of the soul from this world to another. If it is the former, then it is like a deep sleep undisturbed even with dreams, for which we crave when we are alive. If it is the latter, and I am able to go to another world, then I will be able to meet all those good men who lived before me. I will meet Minos, and Rhadamanthus. I will be able to talk to Orpheus. And Musaeus, Hesoid, Homer! Above all, then I would be able to continue my search into truth, without the hindrance of death!

I have but one request to make. When my sons are grown up, I ask you to punish them and trouble them, as I have troubled you, if they seem to care about riches more than about virtue, or if they pretend to possess knowledge, when they don't. Reprove them then, as I have reproved you. If you do this, both I and my sons will have received justice at your hands.

I think the hour of departure to the prison cell has arrived, and we go our ways, I to death and you to life... Which is better, god only knows.

[Light dims on Socrates and comes up on the others.]

THREE: Socrates should have run away then, however hard it was.

CRITO: Hard? It was the easiest thing to do. It was also the custom. They too wished he would. If he died he would be a martyr. That would make life very difficult for them.

THREE: They were bound to think so. That is politics after all.

ONE: But if you look at it from Socrates' point of view, becoming a martyr was the right thing.

CRITO: Socrates would never have done something because it was politically expedient or beneficial. Forget politics. The sentence was unjust. What about that? [*Crito is thinking. Slight pause. He sits down.*] The execution of his sentence was being delayed. We were all worried.

[The others leave. The usual meeting place in the square. Plato enters lost in thought. Crito is irritated, upset. He is pacing up and down. He beats the ground with his cane. A common citizen enters from the left and goes out right.]

CRITO: [*He hits the ground again with his cane. Looking at the man he mutters*] These people should be thrashed. [*The man is startled but continues walking.*]

PLATO: Crito!

CRITO: They call themselves Athenians. Sit on juries.

[Hits the ground with the cane.]

PLATO: Control your anger Crito. He wasn't on the jury.

CRITO: Sure. But does he even know who Socrates is and that he's going to be killed through falsehood? Ask. Ask him. He is a citizen isn't he? Should he not be concerned? Why, why not? If they call themselves citizens...the swine.

[The man starts, looks back once, then exits. Pause]

CRITO: [*Dejected*] When is this city going to wake up? It's all so quiet, inert. As though nothing has happened or is about to happen.

PLATO: People never rise by themselves. They need leaders. Does society ever move on its own?

CRITO: But should they not feel concerned? Have some sense of what's happening? They've turned into statues filled with straw.

[Pause. Alcibiades enters. Clearly he's been drinking but is still in possession of his senses.]

CRITO: Welcome. You were the missing bit.

[Both look at Alcibiades. He sits down. His eyes are wet. He is weeping.]

CRITO: What's the point of crying now? Till the morning of the trial you were talking about bringing Lycon over to our side. [*Alcibiades is silent.*] So tell us how those three came together from three different sides—Anytus, Meletus and Lycon? Together! Would anyone have believed it? And you insiders merely watched. Three men always at each other's throats came together!

PLATO: Don't be childish. An enemy's enemy is a friend. That's as old as the hills. Who would want Socrates around? Nobody.

CRITO: But what were guys like him doing? What was the use of their being there? All they do is drink. Call themselves Senators. What do they do? We depended entirely on Alcibiades to save Socrates.

PLATO: What's the point of blaming him? He must have done his best. But what can you do when the whole system is rotten?

ALCIBIADES: Socrates wouldn't have approved of our efforts. How many things could we do in one day without his knowing?

CRITO: Don't say a word more. Sheds tears now!

ALCIBIADES: [*Suddenly angry*] Why don't you go into politics then? Who has stopped you? Socrates didn't enter politics and that was good. People like him should remain outside. But what about you? You just sit and talk. If nobody like us goes into politics then it will only be Meletus and his...

PLATO: Are we going to fight now?

[Pause]

CRITO: Even Socrates remarked about those three uniting. Even a man like him noticed. That surprises me.

PLATO: Socrates wasn't naïve, Crito. When will you understand simple things?

CRITO: I understand only one thing. He should have been here still.

[Pause]

PLATO: [*Coming forward*] Decisions must be made. Circumstances can't be allowed to decide... But to accept death or run away, this is choosing without a choice—

ALCIBIADES: But he is not even giving a thought to one of them. He is not going to run away... I remember his words whenever I come to this square. I remember his words. His tone. Remember his tone...even the tone is enough to convince one that he is not going to run away! I remember.

CRITO: Oh you do, do you?

PLATO: He's right. What's the point of getting irritated?

CRITO: What is the point of sitting around thinking either? Oracle? That's been done once and this is the result. Even the gods of this place are useless.

PLATO: Crito!

CRITO: You sit and think.

[Pause. Crito calms down a little.]

CRITO: What are you thinking?

PLATO: One day I'm going to start an Academy outside this city. Socrates' ideas must live. Don't laugh.

CRITO: Why should I laugh? Only you can do it. We have gone to seed. Overage. Education for us is like water off a duck's back... Why should this city have come to this pass, Plato? Once this was a city rich in every way. This was the city of men like Pythagoras and Homer. It is now like a crate of rotten fruit.

ALCIBIADES: Don't start an Academy.

CRITO: Why?

ALCIBIADES: It will lead to nothing. Optimists are fools.

PLATO: You've been drinking too much. A lot can still happen in this city. Mark my words.

CRITO: Please do start an Academy. Your mind is exactly like Socrates'. And you are young too.

PLATO: But I still have a lot to learn from Socrates.

CRITO: We'll bring Socrates around. He'll run away with us. The two of you can leave Athens. I have many friends in Thessaly. They will look after you for sure. Learn everything you can. And who knows? This government might even change in six months. And you'll be back.

PLATO: True. Who can tell the future? This government has run out of its store of merit. That is for sure.

CRITO: Come. Let's get down to preparations. My instinct is prompting me. It will take at least three or four days more for the ship to return from Delos. Socrates is safe till then.

PLATO: Who will convince him?

CRITO: I will.

PLATO: It will not be so easy to do. Wait, let us decide what to say...

[Phaedo enters with lowered head and in despair.]

CRITO: [*Runs to him*] What's happened? [*Phaedo does not speak. Shaking him*] What's happened? Speak, fool.

PHAEDO: The ship returns definitely by tomorrow evening. The day after that will be the last.

CRITO: Where were you all this time? Were you simply wandering about with the news?

PHAEDO: I went to Socrates' house.

CRITO: What for? To tell that Xanthippe, that witch.

ALCIBIADES: Crito, she is his wife...

[Pause]

PLATO: What did she say?

PHAEDO: She took the news with great dignity.

CRITO: She could not have felt a thing, having harassed him all his life.

PHAEDO: You should have seen her. Then you would not have said that. She understood Socrates better than any of us.

CRITO: She, a woman?

PLATO: Crito, you are just angry. And anyway, one can hardly expect Athenians to understand women.

CRITO: No problem there.

[Pause. Plato is pacing around. Crito is disturbed.]

CRITO: Are we going to do something or just sit around here.

PLATO: Do something. There is very little time too. Wait here. I will see Xanthippe first. Socrates' children will now be our responsibility. If we have to leave Athens, we will have to take them along.

PHAEDO: I said that to her.

PLATO: And?

PHAEDO: She said that will never happen. Socrates will never run away. Take this as a line etched in stone.

ALCIBIADES: Stupid woman.

PLATO: I will see her again. I will also quickly get in touch with others. Crito, you wait here. Phaedo, Alcibiades, you two go with me.

[*They go. Pause. Crito is alone on the stage. Four enters and sits further away, sunk in his own thoughts. Crito gives him a hard look. Then sits down with head lowered. Gradually Crito finds Four's presence irritating. But he is calm and dejected.*]

CRITO: You are very calm, as though you are looking

down from some cosmic distance. [*Pause*] Are you laughing at our confusion? [*Pause*] Are you not going to speak?

FOUR: Did you think I would laugh at you? [*Momentary silence*] Earlier I did not understand why Meletus should be so scared of Socrates that he would want to see him dead. And now this sepulchral silence that has spread over Athens. As though nothing untoward has happened. This silence even when Socrates' words, so deeply etched on our minds, are repeated to us verbatim. This too I cannot understand.

[One enters and sits down]

FOUR: What did you say and to whom?

CRITO: We spoke to many people. We did not sit around here talking to each other... We talked to many people. Said everything that Socrates used to say. Many wept with us. Many gave us help in our preparations for running away... not that nobody helped... But...

FOUR: But?

CRITO: But to tell the truth...never mind.

[Four laughs]

CRITO: See? You have been wanting to laugh. I wasn't wrong.

FOUR: I did not laugh because of that. I would never dream of mocking you.

CRITO: But you did laugh. [*Pause*] How can Meletus win such an easy victory while we are here?

FOUR: Victory? Is victory the purpose? Surely the purpose is to live righteously.

CRITO: It is necessary sometimes for righteousness and knowledge to win. At least that is how we felt then. Meletus was also staking his all and playing to win.

ONE: [*Interrupting*] But what did you do then? What actually happened?

CRITO: [*Coming to himself*] We were not going to let Meletus win. We made all the necessary preparations as planned and I went to the prison at break of day the next morning. Socrates was asleep like a little child.

[Socrates is asleep at the back. Crito is waiting impatiently for him to wake up. Socrates gets up and is surprised to see Crito.]

SOCRATES: You? At this time? Day is just breaking is it not?

CRITO: It is the first hour of dawn.

SOCRATES: Did the guards allow you in?

CRITO: How many guards do you think there are? Those that are there all know me. They are also obliged to me.

SOCRATES: Have you just come?

CRITO: A little while ago.

SOCRATES: You should have woken me.

CRITO: How peacefully you were sleeping. Even at such a time.

SOCRATES: Should I lose sleep over the idea of death at this age?

CRITO: Many aged people do.

[Socrates laughs. Pause]

CRITO: Yesterday Phaedo and Plato went to your house.

SOCRATES: I have no need to worry when you people are there.

CRITO: Xanthippe does not even need us. She is taking this with equanimity.

SOCRATES: You are telling me?

CRITO: We used to lose our temper over her unnecessarily.

SOCRATES: That was natural. She is a little short-tempered. But she has endured a lot.

CRITO: It's the lot of great men's wives. It is their sacrifice for society.

SOCRATES: [*Laughs*] We say that for the sake of saying it. Why should she suffer? Just because society burdens her with suffering? But her strength is limitless. Even I depended on it many times.

[Pause]

CRITO: We still meet every day.

[Pause]

SOCRATES: Why are you here now Crito? So early? To tell me this?

[Crito is silent.]

SOCRATES: The ship has arrived from Delos. The hour is near. That is what you have come to say.

CRITO: It will arrive today. Tomorrow will be the last day.

SOCRATES: All right.

[Pause]

CRITO: We have made all the arrangements. My friends in Thessaly will be waiting for you and Plato. I have sent them a message yesterday. You need to run away from here.

[Socrates laughs.]

CRITO: Do we not have even this much right over you? Forget about our loss. What will people say? Crito with all his money did not help Socrates to run away. People will spit on us.

SOCRATES: Why should we bother about what people think? Good people will not think that way.

CRITO: We do need to heed people's opinions. You were sentenced to death because of their opinions. Their opinions were responsible for this evil deed.

SOCRATES: I wish this were true. Because if evil deeds result from people's opinions, so should good deeds. How beautiful the world would have been if what you say were true. But the truth is that nothing happens because of their opinions, neither bad nor good. What they do is pure accident. The real reasons and those who cause things to happen are different. Anyway, we should listen only to good and reasonable people and ignore the others. We have proved this often during our conversations.

CRITO: Perhaps. I am not going to argue with you. But still, tell me something. Are you afraid that we will be harassed if you run away? We are strong enough to look after ourselves.

SOCRATES: I'm sure of that.

CRITO: Then what is the reason Socrates? So many people are willing to help you. They are waiting with money in their hands. We have talked to the people to whom the money is to be given. Think of your children. They are still young. You are walking into the enemy's hands. Getting trapped in their stratagems. We should have done this long ago. The trial should not have happened at all. Or we should have organized ourselves differently for it.

SOCRATES: [*Begins to laugh*] Oh but you did try that. Did you think I would not know that you tried to divide Lycon from Meletus? To be outside politics does not mean you don't understand politics. I would have stopped you had I not known that your efforts would fail. There is no credit to being good out of ignorance. The credit lies with being good when you know everything.

CRITO: Even then...

SOCRATES: Crito, being this kind of doer is not always a good thing. I have told you my reasons for not wanting to run away. All my life I have used reason to decide what is right and just. If I change my principles now it will mean I have given in to fear. I will be like children who are afraid of the bogeyman... But for your satisfaction, let us analyse my position. I am standing at the door of death. The mind can become destabilized at times like this. But you are miles away from death. I would like you to answer some questions. If you prove that running away would be the right action, I will give in to you. Otherwise you will have to give in to me. Things like money, what people will say, what will happen to the children have nothing to do with it. Those are considerations to further one's own interests. We will look at one question only. Is it right for me to run away or face death, whoever suffers as a consequence?

CRITO: Sure, I agree, but—

SOCRATES: So tell me, is it right to act falsely, even for a little while and for a good end? All our lives we have said this would be wrong. Have we discovered some new factor that makes it necessary to review this opinion?

CRITO: No.

SOCRATES: Therefore, we must do the right thing whatever the consequences.

CRITO: Yes.

SOCRATES: Is it right to say that the way to demolish sin is by committing a sin?

CRITO: No it isn't. But how would you be sinning by running away? That is what I don't understand and can't accept.

SOCRATES: Let us help you understand by using a device. Suppose the law and the government are standing before me in human form to cross-examine me as I am running away. What will they say? They will say, 'Socrates, what are you doing? By running away you are destroying the entire system. How long will a political system last if people did not care for the law? Are you not trampling the law underfoot by running away?' I know what you want to say Crito. I will say the same thing to them. 'Why should I submit to a legal system that has done me an injustice?'

CRITO: That is precisely what I was thinking.

SOCRATES: To that they will say, 'But had we made a contract that said you would accept only laws that you thought were right and overthrow the rest? You accepted the legal system unconditionally. We helped you grow. Your parents married according to our laws and you were nurtured, educated and won citizen's rights under these very laws. How can you consider yourself equal to us, Socrates? Who gave you the right to behave in a certain way because we have behaved in a certain other way? Would you behave with your parents that way? Would that be considered right behaviour? Should a philosopher not understand that the State is greater even than parents? Whether it is war or the court of justice, you must behave as we decide in every situation. You can change what we decide by reasoning with us. Every citizen has the right to do that. But you cannot take the law in your hands. If you do, you will have to accept whatever punishment is meted out to you.' Now tell me Crito, are they saying something wrong or right?

CRITO: Right.

SOCRATES: They will further say, 'When you came of age we gave you a right that every citizen enjoyed. If you thought we were not right, you were free to leave this city and go anywhere you wished. You cannot do this after so many years because you find it expedient. The fact that you have lived here so many years means you love us. Not only you, your children too were born here. Over and above that, when you were sentenced, you were given the option of paying a fine or be willing to be exiled. You said then that death was preferable to exile. Was that hypocrisy then?' Now tell me, what answer can we make to that?

[Crito is silent]

They will say further, 'And wherever you go, the good people there will look upon you suspiciously as an enemy of the law. All your life you have given first priority to ideas of righteousness and justice. Do not give that up now. Considerations like life and children come later. Whether death is good or bad, whether your ideas about death are right or wrong, running away from it will never give you contentment...' I hear all this Crito like the notes of the flute in the ears of a mystic. Then I can hear nothing else. My way is to change existing conditions, explain to people, search for truth while walking on the path of righteousness. If I am to be punished for that, I must accept the punishment, whatever it is. It would not be right to change my path at such a time. Do you have anything to say to this Crito?

CRITO: No. I accept what you say.

SOCRATES: Go then. Walk on the path that god has shown.

[Socrates falls into thought. Four enters.]

SOCRATES: Come. Sit.

[Pause]

SOCRATES: Say what is in your mind.

FOUR: Do conditions change by adopting this path? They do not. Else the same old questions would not have produced different answers all the time. Why then should I live like this? Why should I be righteous?

[Pause]

SOCRATES: Were you going to live righteously only to change existing conditions? To acquire knowledge and to live accordingly is not merely a means to an end. It is the ultimate end too. Or should be. You can never separate the means from the end. The human soul and brain are never satisfied with eating and drinking alone... It is only when you go beyond them that you become truly human.

FOUR: Is that what culture is?

SOCRATES: Yes. And in human society it is as necessary as food and drink.

FOUR: But now you are talking from the other side as well. From the point of view of society. I don't understand why.

SOCRATES: That is because you cannot separate the individual from society. Do you understand now?

[Pause]

FOUR: Why did you not say this to Crito?

SOCRATES: He knows it.

FOUR: Does he? Then why does he find it so difficult to take a decision? Not only he but the others too? In fact, everybody.

SOCRATES: Because a decision is difficult to make. It is like the creative process.

[Four rises and stands apart. Pause]

SOCRATES: Do you not agree?

FOUR: I do and I don't. In my situation these decisions have become...

SOCRATES: Difficult?

FOUR: Yes.

SOCRATES: Every decision that we make is as difficult as the first one we made. That is true... It happens again and again...I might make a decision. You make exactly the same decision. Even then it is difficult...

[Pause. Four turns his face away. Phaedo and One enter.]

ONE: Were you present Phaedo when Socrates was punished? When he was given poison?

PHAEDO: Yes, I was.

FOUR: Please tell me about it. Were you alone?

PHAEDO: We were all there, the usual group. There were

many others too. He spoke about philosophy for a long time. We were all there. Only Plato wasn't. He was not well.

TWO: Tell us about the whole thing in detail.

PHAEDO: I will. When we arrived, his chains were being removed. He was told that the death sentence would be carried out at sunset. Xanthippe was there earlier.

[Light only on Socrates and Xanthippe.]

SOCRATES: Crito was here yesterday.

XANTHIPPE: H'm.

SOCRATES: Wanted me to run away.

XANTHIPPE: H'm.

SOCRATES: He said he had been over to our place.

XANTHIPPE: H'm.

SOCRATES: Did you tell him I would never run away?

XANTHIPPE: Yes.

[Pause]

SOCRATES: Why did we not come this close during our life together? I knew you and yet I did not.

XANTHIPPE: I, too, was such a scold, always complaining. Everybody hates me. It is my fault.

SOCRATES: No Xanthippe. I should have made more efforts to make you understand. It should have happened long ago. [*Pause*] The difference in our ages was an obstacle.

XANTHIPPE: Let us find satisfaction in saying that.

SOCRATES: Meaning?

XANTHIPPE: Nothing.

SOCRATES: Speak. Don't keep anything back now. Don't keep me in suspense at such a time.

XANTHIPPE: The difference in age did matter. And... It was not as though I found your way of life, your philosophy unacceptable. But two individuals cannot be the same. Philosophy should be open enough to include every kind of person. An ideology cannot consider itself complete merely by satisfying a single individual's mind and ideas.

SOCRATES: Xanthippe!

XANTHIPPE: It surprises you to hear me speak in this language? I've been listening to you closely for all these years.

SOCRATES: Speak on. Don't stop now.

XANTHIPPE: Must one live in rags when one accepts your philosophy? Must my children never eat a single good thing in their lives? This society brings up women in such a way that they remain tied to the soil. Naturally they think of material things. But our materialism is real. Genuine. Deep. We are concerned about our children. I was not asking to live in a palace. But these ideas don't have a place in your philosophy.

SOCRATES: Xanthippe, we feel we have found the truth. It is right there. And then it slips through our fingers. Did I go wrong?

XANTHIPPE: How can I of all people say you were wrong? I do not have that authority. You were obliged to stick to your principles. It must always be like that. I would also constantly quarrel with you in the other extreme. I didn't speak my mind clearly to you, did I? You grew in stature. Became remote. I could never reach you. But that doesn't mean I didn't understand you at all.

SOCRATES: Every philosophy should aim to be inclusive. That is true. It is equally true that it should make no compromises. Perhaps this idea of not compromising keeps a person's vision locked up within himself.

[Xanthippe says nothing. She cannot repress a sob.]

SOCRATES: Perhaps you should go home now Xanthippe.

[She rises and goes away. Crito, Alcibiades etc enter.]

SOCRATES: Crito, Xanthippe...

CRITO: Xanthippe what?

SOCRATES: Never mind. My mind cannot grasp everything. That is the truth. I must keep searching for the truth and stay true to what I have understood. I will perhaps continue to make mistakes although there is little time left for that.

CRITO: Meaning?

[Pause]

CRITO: We will take good care of Xanthippe and the children.

SOCRATES: I have no doubts about that. Perhaps there is not much need for that either.

[Long pause. It is obvious that Socrates is trying resolutely to put Xanthippe out of his mind. Light again on Phaedo.]

PHAEDO: Socrates was silent for a while, rubbing his hands and feet which had been just released from chains. He looked lost. Then he spoke of many things. At one moment we were full of joy to hear him talk and the next moment deep in sorrow at the thought of his death. He was talking the whole day. About death. About suicide. About the body and the soul. How only the soul can acquire pure knowledge and how the knowledge that comes through emotions can be deceptive. He explained why righteousness and knowledge cannot be separated. He spoke of ideas that stand opposed to each other. He spoke at great length.

[Pause]

FOUR: Why are you silent?

PHAEDO: I was remembering the question Crito asked.

[The whole stage is now in light. Socrates is in the prison surrounded by the others.]

CRITO: Do you have any last instructions for us Socrates? About your children?

SOCRATES: Nothing special. Take care of yourselves. Do not stray from your path.

CRITO: Anything about how you'd like to be buried?

SOCRATES: Keep a tight hold of me after I die to make sure I don't run away. [*Laughs*] Nothing I can say will convince him. What will die is my body. Socrates will be on his way. None of you need wait here after my death. You will suffer anguish I know. You will sit here saying, 'We are giving Socrates eternal rest.' Or some such thing. False words are not only bad in themselves but they also corrupt the soul without our knowledge. Keep calm. Tell yourselves that my body has been interred. Do what is routinely done. I have no special instructions to give.

PHAEDO: Then he got up and went with Crito to have a bath. We sat numbed. Some were talking to each other about the things he had said. Others just sat. A little while later he said goodbye to his eldest sons outside and then came in to sit with us. The hour of sunset was near. The jail warden entered.

WARDEN: This evil job always falls to my lot. But I am certain Socrates that you will not be like the others. You will not rave and rant and curse me. You are different. What can I say? I am under obligation to obey orders. The poison is ready. I'll bring it in when you're ready. Please forgive me.

[He goes out sobbing.]

SOCRATES: [*Indicating the warden as he leaves*] See how we sometimes chance upon good people. How can I repay you for your goodness? What a transparent mind he has.

He used to visit me every day. He would inquire after me. And now he is sad for me. Crito, there is no point in wasting time now. Please fetch the poison.

CRITO: But there's time yet for the sun to set. Shall I get you something else before that? Other people don't even keep to the sunset hour. Please don't hurry. Everybody is given that much leeway.

SOCRATES: I am aware that people delay things. They are not wrong. They want to extend life a little. But you know very well that is not what I want. To delay in my case is pure foolishness. Please do as I said.

[Crito makes a gesture. The warden comes in with the poison. Socrates takes it from him.]

SOCRATES: You have a lot of experience with this. Can you tell me how I can die peacefully?

WARDEN: I will give you a tip. Keep walking after you've drunk the poison. It helps the poison to circulate. Keep walking till your legs feel heavy. Then lie down on the ground. The poison will do its work.

[Socrates drinks the poison without any emotion. Everybody turns away, sobbing noiselessly. Socrates paces the floor. Somebody's sob breaks out. The others look at him confused, angry.]

SOCRATES: [*Momentarily stopping in his tracks*] What was that strange noise? I sent the women home because I did not want them to see this. I believe a man should die in peace. Please keep a hold on yourselves. Be calm.

[The people quieten down, ashamed. Socrates continues to walk for a little while longer. Then he lies down on his back. Pause. The warden looks at his feet and presses them hard.]

WARDEN: Can you feel me pressing your feet?

SOCRATES: No. [*Socrates pulls the cover on his body up over his head. The warden now presses his hand. Pause. Socrates removes the cover from his face for a few moments.*]

SOCRATES: [*In a calm voice*] Crito, I owe Aslepius a fowl. Will you take it to him for me?

CRITO: It will reach him immediately. Anything else?

[The question remains unanswered. Socrates makes a slight movement after a minute. The cover on his body is removed. Crito closes his eyes. The shadows of all the people gathered there are thrown against the wall like the shadows in the cave. Everybody stands still, as though nailed to the spot. Only Four has walked away, focused. The light is on him alone for a while. Then it fades out.]

Curtain

Acknowledgements

The publication of this collection has been partially funded by a grant from Praj Foundation.